VEGETARIAN WORLD FOOD

VEGETARIAN WORLD FOOD

KURMA DASA

CHAKRA PRESS

CHAKRA PRESS
10 Rochester Street, Botany, New South Wales 2019, Australia
e-mail: austbbt@attglobal.net
www.krishna.com

ISBN 0 9578345 1 9

Dedication

In 1969, my Spiritual Master, His Divine Grace Srila A.C Bhaktivedanta Swami Prabhupada, wrote to his young disciple Krishna Devi:

"I am pleased to learn that you are thinking of putting together a cookbook of our recipes. I understand that in London, Yamuna Dasi has already done some work on this same project, so you may correspond with her in his connection. I know that at our feasts especially many persons become interested in preparing foodstuffs in this way, so this cookbook is a nice thing to instruct such persons in preparing and offering nice prasadam (sanctified vegetarian food). I am pleased to note your description of the increasing interest in vegetarian diet. Actually, the practice of meat-eating is very detrimental to spiritual life, and meat-eating means simply to force oneself to suffer the reactions of killing our fellow living entities. So, as many people will be taking to practicing spiritual life, such a cookbook will be very important . . ."

Krishna Devi and Yamuna both went on to write cookbooks. Yamuna's books, especially *The Art of Indian Vegetarian Cooking*, have become award-winning best sellers. As Prabhupada predicted over 30 years ago, many people have indeed taken up a more spiritual way of life, a life that is explicitly linked to being a vegetarian.

This, my fourth cookbook, is thus presented as a humble offering for the pleasure of Srila Prabhupada and for all who are eager to tread more lightly on our planet Earth.

Acknowledgments

I would like to offer my thanks to the following persons who have contributed to this book:

Naresvara Dasa, Matt Roots, Peter Bailey, Peter Colville, Susan Whitter, Maureen McKeon, Jane Borthwick, Carol D'Costa, F. Wit and Jesse.

CONTENTS

Introduction

People often ask how I first became involved in cooking. Have I always cooked vegetarian food? Was I born a vegetarian? The answer is that my involvement in a vegetarian lifestyle, cooking, and my hunger for a more spiritual way of life all began at the same time — in my last year of high school in 1970.

As a student at Vaucluse Boys High School in Sydney, Australia, I found myself inexplicably drawn to all things Indian. I would read books on yoga and mysticism, listen to Indian music, burn incense and buy Indian clothes. I had just become a vegetarian and enjoyed the taste of Indian food. So when my best friend, Mark, invited me to a newly-opened Hare Krishna temple in Paddington, Sydney, I jumped at the chance.

I had heard of Hare Krishna, but knew very little about it. I recalled first hearing the words 'Hare Krishna' in the Beatles song 'I Am the Walrus', and then on George Harrison's famous single 'Radha Krishna Temple' released on Apple label. Mark and I had gone along to see the newly-opened musical 'Hair' at the Metro Theatre in Kings Cross only months before.

At the rousing incense-filled finale, the whole audience (except me) had stood and chanted Hare Krishna along with the cast. Despite the fact that I was too shy to join in, the mantra had stuck in my mind. But, apart from that, I knew nothing about the Hare Krishnas.

We entered the quaint little shop-front filled with incense smoke. After sitting through a lecture on the *Bhagavad-gita,* we were served refreshments — slices of orange, dried figs and little cups of nutmeg and banana-infused warm milk. The philosophy had not really sunk in, but the taste of the food sure did — I had never tasted anything so delicious. A young English girl in a sari invited us back on Sunday to what she called 'The Love Feast'. During the next few days I could not get the taste of that food out of my mind.

At the feast on Sunday there were more taste sensations. Mark and I sat cross-legged, along with about fifty other first-timers, and savoured the new, exciting flavours. There were numerous dishes, but the two that remain in my mind were the warm, firm buttery pudding (made from semolina) called halava, and slices of eggplant dipped in a spicy chickpea flour batter and fried in ghee.

I started to make regular visits to the temple after school. One evening, a saffron-robed monk called Upananda invited me to assist him in the dimly-lit temple kitchen. He was rolling small balls of soft, milky-coloured dough that were to become a sweet called *gulab jamuns.* The task was a long one — at least two hours — but the time went fast as Upananda regaled me with the fascinating story of what we were doing in that tiny basement kitchen and why.

Shaven-headed Upananda had not long before been long-haired Bill Willis and had started reading mystical literature at a psychedelic book shop in Berkeley, California, at the end of 1969. One day, in return for a small donation, Bill received a card with the mantra and a message on it from a monk on Telegraph Avenue. The card had read:

Please chant:

> *Hare Krishna, Hare Krishna*
> *Krishna Krishna, Hare Hare*
> *Hare Rama, Hare Rama*
> *Rama Rama, Hare Hare*

And your life will be sublime.

Bill had started chanting straight away, eager to experience the promised sublimity. Increasingly disgruntled with the shallow, hedonistic life of drugs and sex, Bill accepted his father's offer of a free ticket anywhere in the world. Now a vegetarian and macrobiotic, Bill decided to head to Hawaii, Auckland and then Sydney.

Renting a flat in Sydney's Kings Cross, Bill one day caught sight of a Hare Krishna monk. As they both crossed paths, the devotee smiled warmly and said "Hare Krishna".

They talked, and the devotee, who introduced himself as Upendra, invited Bill to their temple. He started visiting the temple daily and was impressed by Upendra's convincing presentation of the Krishna Consciousness philosophy. Not long after, Bill moved into the temple and received the new name Upananda.

As the saffron-clad chef told me his tale, I found the Sanskrit names a bit confusing and became mixed up between Upendra and Upananda. "Who was Upendra," I asked, "and what was he doing in Kings Cross in the first place?"

Before he continued the story, Upananda directed me to lower the balls of dough into the large pan of warm clarified butter, called ghee, and requested me to help him gently stir them.

As we methodically stirred the golden balls, Upananda explained that Upendra and another devotee, Bali Mardan, had come to Australia on the request of their guru — whose name was A.C. Bhaktivedanta Swami Prabhupada. Upananda referred to him during the rest of our conversation by his shorter title of 'Prabhupada'.

Prabhupada had been asked by his guru to spread the teachings of India's classic *Bhagavad-gita* in the West. Prabhupada had established a small shop-front temple in New York four years previously in 1966. Since then, the Hare Krishna movement had spread rapidly around the world and had taken root in Sydney due to the pioneering efforts of Upendra and his companion.

The balls by this time had become quite dark in colour, so Upananda showed me how to lift them, one by one, out of the ghee with a slotted spoon, and put them to soak in thick sugar syrup.

The first tiny temple had been in Potts Point, a suburb close to Kings Cross, Upananda explained. In their spare time, Bali Mardan and Upendra used to chant with drums and cymbals in the Domain, a vast, well-kept expanse of parkland dotted with sprawling old fig trees near the city.

The Domain was well known as a 'Park for the People', coming to life every Sunday afternoon, offering instant crowds that eagerly gathered around anyone who had something to say. Philosophers, evangelists, political activists and popular heroes would proselytise atop ladders, in the same way as in 'Speakers' Corner' at London's Hyde Park.

After chanting and addressing the Domain crowd for some time, Bali Mardan or Upendra would extend an open invitation to the crowd to return with them to the charming old temple at Potts Point for a 'Love Feast'.

Upendra had been personally taught to cook by Prabhupada, and Upendra had taught Upananda. And now Upananda was teaching me! "What an honour," I thought.

By now the *gulab jamuns* were soaking in their thick syrup. Upananda poured in a good quantity of highly-scented rose water, filling the kitchen with a divine fragrance. The sweets looked good enough to eat right now, I thought, but Upananda seemed to read my mind. "No," he explained, "these are for the 'Love Feast' on Sunday."

Prabhupada had originally adopted the name 'Love Feast' back in 1966, and he had told the devotees that such feasts for the public should become an important part of the Hare Krishna movement.

"Vegetarian food offered to Krishna becomes spiritual," Upananda said, "and whoever eats the food — called *prasadam* — receives great spiritual benefit."

What Upananda said next really impressed me. "This cooking is actually called *bhakti-yoga,* the yoga of love," he said. "Giving people spiritual life in the form of delicious pure vegetarian food cooked with love is what *bhakti-yoga* is all about."

One of the main elements of *bhakti-yoga,* Upananda pointed out, was the preparation of sacred foods, foods fit for God. For thousands of years, priests in temples through-out India had prepared divine vegetarian offerings for the Supreme Being, known by names such as Krishna and Rama. These offerings were saturated with love and devotion.

The Sanskrit word 'yoga' means 'connection', specifically the connection between the individual soul and the Supreme Soul. That connection had now been broken, and yoga was the means for re-establishing it.

The connection between the soul and Supreme Soul was intimate and personal, and the techniques for re-establishing the connection were also intimate and personal.

"If we love someone, we want to do things for them, and a very common thing that people do for people they love is to cook for them," said Upananda.

"Practitioners of *bhakti-yoga* prepare offerings for Krishna in this same spirit of love. This love is manifested at every stage of the cooking process — from the purchasing of the ingredients to the final offering of the sacred meal to the object of one's devotion."

I thought it all sounded profound, yet vey reasonable. I went home and thought deeply about what Upananda had said.

That day in the kitchen was an eventful one. A few months later I had shaved my head and was living in the temple as a full-time monk. I became a disciple of Prabhupada in 1971 and received the name Kurma Dasa. It wasn't long before I was cooking full-time in the kitchen and preparing my own feasts. And the rest is history.

It's thirty years later, and I no longer live in a temple. I don't shave my head (don't need to, as the ageing process has taken care of that!) but the practices of *bhakti-yoga* are still pivotal in my life. I write and teach and cook and chant, and enjoy kitchen life more than ever.

This book is offered in gratitude to all those who have enjoyed my cooking over the years. My heartfelt thanks to these and to all my new friends who are encountering this cuisine for the first time. The recipes selected for inclusion in *Vegetarian World Food* are personal favourites. I do hope you enjoy this book.

Hare Krishna — and happy eating!

Kurma Dasa
26 December 2001
Perth, Western Australia

How to Measure and Use the Recipes

MEASUREMENT OF VOLUME
To conveniently use these recipes, you will require a set of graduated spoons (¼ teaspoon, ½ teaspoon, 1 teaspoon and 1 tablespoon) and a set of graduated cups (¼ cup, ⅓ cup, ½ cup and 1 cup). A glass or plastic liquid measuring container, usually containing cup pint and litre markings will also be handy. Note that there is some difference between Australian, American and British cup and spoon measurements, as explained below.

Teaspoons: Australian, American and British teaspoons all hold approximately 5ml.

Tablespoons: tablespoon measurements given in this book are standard Australian tablespoons, holding 20ml. The American standard tablespoon holds 14.2ml and the British standard tablespoon holds 17.7ml. American readers are advised to heat their tablespoons and British readers to slightly heap their tablespoons.

Cups: cup measurements given in this book are standard Australian cups, which hold 250ml. The American and British cups hold 240ml. Thus American and British readers should generously fill their standard measuring cups, and in the case of liquids, should add 2 teaspoons extra for every cup required.

MEASUREMENT OF WEIGHT
All measurements of weight in this book have been given in metric with imperial in brackets.
Thus: 140g (5 ounces) butter

MEASUREMENT OF TEMPERATURE
Accurate temperatures are indicated for baking and for some deep-frying. In this book, measurements are given first in Celsius, then in Fahrenheit. Thus: 185°C/365°F A cooking thermometer is a useful accessory.

Baking: all recipes were tested in a fan-forced electric oven. If you are baking in a conventional oven, add on approximately 5 minutes to the baking times.

MEASUREMENT OF LENGTH
Measurements are given in centimetres with inches in parentheses.
Thus: 1.25cm (½-inch)
      25cm (10 inches)

IN CONCLUSION
Take note of the following suggestions to get the best out of these recipes:
• Read the entire recipe first and obtain all the ingredients before commencing to cook. Measure all the ingredients beforehand and place them where they can be easily reached.
• All measurements for the spoons and cups are level unless other wise specified.

• For information about unfamiliar ingredients or techniques, see Glossary.

SPECIAL NOTES FOR AMERICAN COOKS
The following list will clarify any confusion that may arise because of the different cooking terms and ingredient names used in Australia and America.

baking tray	baking sheet
beetroot	beet
bicarbonate of soda	baking soda
biscuit	cookie
cake tin	cake/baking pan
capsicums	peppers
caster sugar	fine granulated sugar
chickpeas	garbanzo beans
continental parley	flat-leaf parsley
cornflour	corn starch
frying pan	skillet
grill	broil
icing sugar	confectioner's sugar
plain flour	all-purpose flour
raw sugar	turbinado sugar
self-raising flour	self-rising flour
semolina	farina
sultanas	golden raisins
wholemeal flour	wholewheat flour

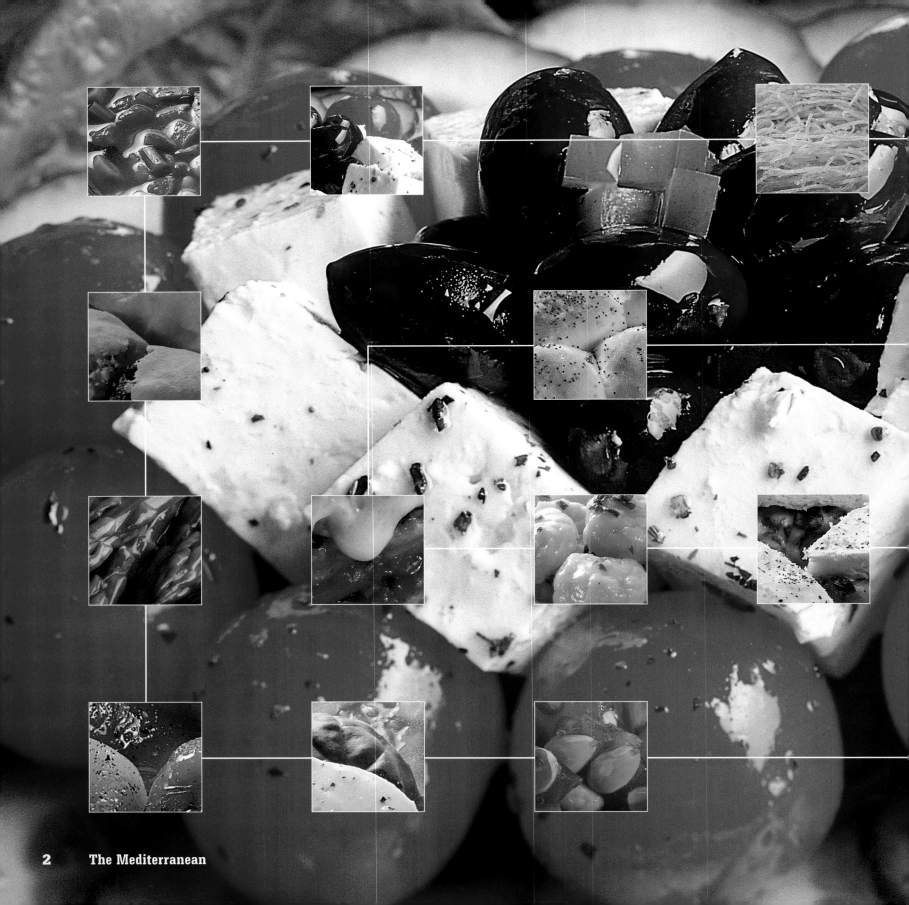

THE MEDITERRANEAN

There's nothing like a steaming pot of hot soup to warm you up on a cold winter's day, and this one "does the trick". Probably every Greek housewife has a version of fasoulada, a full-bodied, thick rustic soup of white beans and vegetables. Any white beans are preferred, such as cannellini, black-eyed beans, lima, navy or haricot. You can serve fasoulada as an entrée, or you can build a substantial meal around it by adding bread, olives and cheese.

Preparation & cooking time:
about 1 hour

Bean soaking time:
1 hour or overnight

Serves: 6 persons

- 2 cups haricot beans or white beans of your choice, soaked overnight
- 1 teaspoon yellow asafetida powder
- 1½ cups chopped, peeled tomatoes
- ¾ cup diced carrot
- 1 cup chopped celery, including leaves
- 2 tablespoons tomato paste
- ¼ cup chopped parsley
- 2-3 tablespoons virgin olive oil
- ¼ teaspoon freshly-ground black pepper
- ½ teaspoon sugar
- 1½ teaspoons salt
- chopped parsley for garnish

Greek-style White Bean & Vegetable Soup
Fasoulada

Drain and rinse the soaked beans. Place them in a 5-litre/quart saucepan along with about 8 cups fresh water, and bring to the boil over full heat.

Add all the other ingredients to the saucepan, except the salt and garnish. Return the pan to full heat, bring to the boil, then reduce the heat to a simmer, and cook, tightly covered, for about 1 hour, or until the beans are soft.

Stir in the salt and sprinkle each bowl of hot steaming soup with some of the reserved parsley. Succulent!

*S*mall, bun-sized pieces of herbed and yeasted dough are arranged in a quiche pan or shallow cake tin fairly close together, then baked. They come to the table joined together in a singular circular cluster, and diners can break off a roll as desired.

Herbed Bread Rolls

Combine the yeast, a few teaspoons of warm water, and the sugar in a small bowl. Set aside for 10 minutes, or until the mixture is frothy.

Whisk together the flour and salt. Add the oil, herbs and yellow asafetida powder to the frothy yeast mixture. Make a well in the centre of the flour and pour in the yeast mixture. Add three-quarters of the warm water, and mix. Add enough of the remaining water, if required, to make a soft but non-sticky dough.

Knead the dough for 5-8 minutes. Place the dough in an oiled bowl, cover with plastic wrap and leave in a warm place for one hour, or until doubled in bulk.

Punch down the dough and divide into 18 even-sized pieces. Shape them by rolling them around under cupped hands on a floured board or marble slab, then arrange them fairly close together in a lightly oiled, 25cm (10-inch) quiche pan or round, shallow baking dish. Keep in mind that the rolls will approximately double in size. Allow the rolls to rise again for about 30 minutes. Spray with water and sprinkle with poppy seeds, sesame, fine oatmeal or dried herbs.

Pre-heat the oven to 220°C/430°F.

Bake the rolls for 30-35 minutes or until golden brown and hollow-sounding when tapped on the base. Serve as described above.

Preparation & baking time: about 1 hour

Dough resting time:
First rise: 1 hour.
Second rise: 30 minutes

Makes: 18 rolls

- 1 teaspoon dried yeast
- about 1¼ cups warm water
- 1 teaspoon sugar
- 3 cups plain unbleached bread flour
- 1 teaspoon salt
- 3 teaspoons oil
- 1 teaspoon fresh thyme leaves, chopped
- 1 teaspoon fresh oregano leaves, chopped
- 2 teaspoons fresh basil leaves, chopped
- ½ teaspoon yellow asafetida powder
- poppy seeds, sesame seeds, fine oatmeal or dried herbs for topping

Preparation & baking time:
about 1 hour 10 minutes

Dough resting time:
45 minutes

Makes: 1 thick 25cm (10-inch) bread

The dough

- 2 teaspoons dried yeast
- 1 cup warm water
- ½ teaspoon sugar
- 3 cups unbleached plain bread flour
- 1 teaspoon yellow asafetida powder
- ½ teaspoon salt
- 4 tablespoons olive oil

The filling

- 2 cups grated cheddar cheese
- 2 cups grated mozzarella cheese
- ½ cup freshly grated Parmesan cheese
- ½-¾ cup halved or chopped kalamata olives
- packed ½ cup coarsely chopped oil-packed sundried tomatoes
- packed ½ cup chopped fresh basil leaves
- 1-2 tablespoons oil from sun dried tomatoes
- ½ teaspoon freshly-ground black pepper

Focaccia has become a national dish of Italy, and many regional versions can be found, all quite different. My version is probably a cross between the local country cuisine of the Puglia region, where breads are enriched with the ingredients of the pastoral people such as tomatoes, herbs and oil, and southern versions adding cheese. This recipe makes a large thick focaccia (it can only just be called a "flat bread") filled with a variety of tasty, herby, melty mouth-watering ingredients. Serve focaccia hot from the oven for a taste treat.

Stuffed Italian Flat bread
Focaccia

The topping

- a little olive oil for brushing on the bread
- dried basil for sprinkling
- coarse sea salt (optional)

Sift the flour, yellow asafetida powder and salt into a large bowl. Pour in the frothy yeast mixture, the olive oil and the remaining water. Mix well.

Knead on a floured surface for about 8-10 minutes, or until the dough is velvety and

Stir the dried yeast into ¼ cup of the warm water. Sprinkle in the sugar and leave in a warm place for about 10 minutes, or until frothy.

soft. Place the dough in a lightly oiled bowl and cover the bowl with oiled plastic wrap. Leave the dough in a warm, draught-free place for about 45 minutes, or until doubled in size.

Punch the dough down and remove it from the bowl. Place it on a lightly floured surface and knead it briefly. Divide the dough into two equal portions. Roll out one portion to a 25cm (10-inch) round disk and place it on a well-oiled baking sheet.

Sprinkle on half the cheeses, leaving a 1.25cm (½-inch) border of dough. Evenly cover the cheese with the olives, sun

Note: For variety, or just plain indulgence, try adding one or more of the following ingredients to the focaccia filling: 1-2 cups thinly-sliced grilled or pan-fried zucchini, 1-2 cups steamed or pan-fried tender asparagus, 1-2 cups capsicum (pepper) strips, 1-2 cups grilled or pan-fried eggplant slices, 1-2 cups marinated artichoke hearts.

dried tomatoes and basil leaves. Drizzle over the oil from the sun dried tomatoes, and sprinkle on the black pepper. Cover with the remaining cheese. Moisten the outer border of exposed dough with water.

Pre-heat the oven to 220°C/430°F.

Roll out the other portion of dough to exactly the same size and carefully lift it on top of the filled base. Tightly seal the top to the bottom, making sure no filling is exposed. Brush the surface of the focaccia with olive oil, sprinkle with basil and the optional sea salt. Place the focaccia in the centre of the pre-heated oven.

Bake for 30 minutes, or until the top is golden brown. Remove and carefully place the bread on a rack to cool, or cut into wedges and serve immediately.

This is a typical dish from the Veneto region of northern Italy. Its beauty lies in its simplicity. Serve this dish as antipasto (entrée).

Asparagus with Oil & Lemon Sauce

Preparation & cooking time: 20 minutes

Serves: 4 persons

- 2 bunches of fresh asparagus, 500g (a little over 1 pound) trimmed
- juice of 1 lemon
- 3 tablespoons olive oil
- ½ teaspoon salt
- ¼ teaspoon freshly ground black pepper
- ¼ teaspoon freshly grated nutmeg
- 2-4 tablespoons grated Parmesan cheese

Tie the asparagus in a bundle and stand it in a tall pot in 5cm (2-inches) water. Cover the pot and allow the asparagus to boil gently over moderate heat until the stems are cooked but still a little firm (about 5 minutes). Alternatively, place the asparagus in a steamer.

Serve: place the asparagus on a warmed serving dish. Mix the lemon juice, oil, salt, pepper, and nutmeg, pour this sauce over the hot asparagus, and sprinkle with cheese. Serve immediately.

*R*oasted peppers (capsicums), sprinkled with salt and covered with fragrant olive oil make an ideal antipasto. They are also a perfect accompaniment to a casual lunch. Roasting your own peppers is far more rewarding — and economical — than purchasing ready-made jars from the supermarket. Home-roasted peppers last at least a week if stored under oil and longer if kept in the refrigerator.

Roasted Sweet Peppers in Olive Oil

Insalata di Peperoni Arrostiti

Preparation & cooking time:
20 minutes

Serves: 6 persons

- 6 large fleshy red peppers, or a combination of red, yellow and green
- salt and pepper to taste
- 4 tablespoons extra-virgin olive oil

Slice the peppers in half lengthways. Remove the membranes, stalk and seeds. Lay the peppers cut-side down on a baking sheet.

Grill under a hot griller for 10 minutes, or until blackened and blistered.

Transfer the peppers into a plastic bag. Close tightly and leave for 20 minutes. This steaming will help loosen the skins.

Remove the peppers from the bag, and peel off their skin. Holding the peppers under cold running water while doing this helps speed up the process. Sprinkle with salt and pepper and drizzle with olive oil.

Serve at room temperature.

Note: If you don't have a griller, you can roast your peppers in a hot oven (200°C/390°F) for about 30 minutes. If you don't have either an oven or a griller, place the peppers over a naked gas flame, turning with a pair of kitchen tongs until the peppers are blackened and blistered, then proceed as above.

**Preparation time:
20 minutes**

Serves: 6-8 persons

- 1 medium crisp Cos or Iceberg lettuce
- ⅔ cup olive oil
- ½ cup fresh lemon juice
- 1 teaspoon salt
- ½ teaspoon freshly ground black pepper
- 500g (a little over 1 pound) feta cheese cut into 1.5cm (½-inch) cubes
- 1 tablespoon dried oregano
- 1 medium cucumber, unpeeled, sliced into 0.5cm (¼-inch) rings
- 500g (a little over 1 pound) whole cherry tomatoes
- 250g (9 ounces) Greek black olives (try Kalamata)
- 1 small green pepper, seeded and sliced into 0.5cm (¼-inch) rings

A Greek salad is not tossed but carefully constructed, making an attractive centre-piece at a buffet lunch or dinner. This stunning salad features feta cheese and Greek black olives, both available from continental grocers. This salad is not served on individual plates but, following Greek style, is dismantled piece by piece, smorgasbord style, by the guests.

Greek Salad

Line a large oblong platter with the outer leaves of a crisp head of lettuce. Tear the remaining leaves into small pieces; season them with a quarter of the olive oil, half the lemon juice, and half of the salt and pepper. Arrange the lettuce on the platter.

Pour another quarter of the olive oil and half the oregano on the feta cheese cubes.

Salt and pepper the cucumber slices. Place the cucumbers in an overlapping ring around the outer perimeter of the platter.

Arrange three-quarters of the cherry tomatoes among the cucumber slices.

Place a ring of feta cheese and half the olives inside the ring of cucumber. Pile the remaining cherry tomatoes in the centre along with the remaining black olives.

Decorate the centrepiece with the slices of pepper and pour the remaining lemon and oil on the salad, garnishing it with the remaining salt, pepper, and oregano.

I tasted this ultra-delicious combination of fresh buffalo-milk mozzarella cheese, slices of ripe tomatoes and fresh basil leaves for the first time while in Rome. The pure white mozzarella had been literally made fresh that morning and came floating in whey in little plastic bags. For the best results, select the freshest mozzarella and basil leaves, aromatic virgin olive oil and vine ripe tomatoes.

Tomato, Basil & Fresh Mozzarella Salad

Insalata Caprese

Preparation time: a few minutes

Serves: 4 persons

- 250g (9 ounces) buffalo-milk mozzarella balls or bocconcini, thinly sliced
- a few fresh basil leaves, shredded, for garnish
- 3 or 4 medium-sized ripe roma tomatoes thinly sliced
- sea salt
- coarsely-ground black pepper
- 2-3 tablespoons extra virgin olive oil
- 12-15 whole large fresh basil leaves

Arrange the slices of cheese, whole basil leaves and tomato slices in decorative overlapping rings on a serving platter.

Serve: just before serving, sprinkle over the salt, the black pepper, drizzle with the extra virgin olive oil and garnish with the shredded basil leaves.

Preparation & cooking time: about 15 minutes

Serves: 4-6 persons

- 1½ cups yellow button squash cut into wedges or sections
- 1½ cups sliced green beans
- 1½ cups cauliflower cut into medium-sized florets
- 1½ cups broccoli cut into medium-sized florets
- 1½ cups zucchini cut into wedges
- leaves from half bunch silverbeet (Swiss chard), slightly blanched in boiling water and drained

Greek-style Oil & Lemon Dressing

- ½ cup olive oil
- ¼ cup lemon juice
- 1 tablespoon rigani, or 2 tablespoons fresh oregano leaves, chopped
- ¼ teaspoon yellow asafetida powder
- ½ teaspoon salt
- ½ teaspoon freshly-ground black pepper

*G*reek oregano, rigani, is a stronger, sharper version of the familiar Italian herb. The word oregano derives from the Greek, meaning "joy of the mountains", and was well-known to the ancient Greeks. Today it covers the hills and mountain slopes of Greece, perfuming the air with its flavour. You can find bunches of dried rigani in Continental stores; it is worth seeking out to give an authentic flavour to the traditional latholemono dressing that goes with this very palatable warm vegetable salad — a delicious meal in itself when accompanied by crusty bread.

Warm Vegetable Salad with Greek-style Oil & Lemon Dressing

Lightly cook the vegetables in slightly salted water until just tender. Briefly blanch the silverbeet leaves in the water.

Drain the vegetables thoroughly.

Arrange the hot vegetables on a bed of the slightly blanched silverbeet leaves on the platter you wish to serve them.

Greek-style Oil & Lemon Dressing
Combine all the ingredients in a screw-top jar, seal and shake well or combine in a bowl and whisk.

Pour the dressing on top of the vegetables.

Serve immediately.

Genoa, Northern Italy, is the home of the famous "Pasta Pesto alla Genovese" with a pungent sauce called "pesto", made primarily of fresh basil leaves, Parmesan cheese, and toasted pine nuts. Traditionally, ribbon-shaped pasta such as trenette or linguine are used.

Pasta Pesto

Crush the basil with the salt and half the olive oil in a large pestle and mortar, or in a food processor. Add the rest of the olive oil, the asafetida, pine nuts and three-quarters of the cheese. Blend until smooth. Add a little water if too thick.

Cook the pasta in plenty of salted boiling water until cooked but still a little firm (al dente). Drain thoroughly.

Serve immediately with the pesto sauce.

- **Preparation & cooking time:**
  20 minutes
- **Serves: 6 persons**
- 1½ cups chopped fresh basil leaves
- 1 teaspoon salt
- ½ cup olive oil
- 3 tablespoons pine nuts lightly toasted and chopped
- ¾ teaspoon yellow asafetida powder
- 125g (4 ounces) grated Parmesan cheese
- 500g (a little over 1 pound) pasta trenette or pasta linguine

*S*ouvlaki is a well-known grilled meat dish from Greece that is sometimes served wrapped in flat breads. Here's a vegetarian version.

Grilled Vegetables Wrapped in Pita Breads

Souvlakia

**Preparation & cooking time:
45 minutes**

Makes: 8 souvlakia

- 4 long thin eggplants cut into 2cm (¾-inch) rounds
- 2 medium zucchinis cut into 2cm (¾-inch) rounds
- 8 firm plum tomatoes, cut in half lengthways, seeds squeezed out
- 1 large green capsicum (pepper) cut into 12 pieces
- 1 large red capsicum (pepper) cut into 12 pieces

Marinade

- 1 teaspoon yellow asafetida powder
- ⅓ cup olive oil
- 2 tablespoons balsamic vinegar or lemon juice
- 1 teaspoon dried oregano or thyme
- 2 teaspoons salt
- 1 teaspoon freshly-ground black pepper

Sauce

- 1 cup Greek yogurt, preferably drained overnight
- 1 tablespoon olive oil
- ½ teaspoon yellow asafetida powder
- ½ teaspoon salt
- ¼ teaspoon freshly-ground black pepper
- 1 teaspoon sweet paprika
- extra 2 tablespoons olive oil
- 8 pita breads

Combine all the cut vegetables in a large bowl. Whisk the marinade ingredients together in a small bowl, and pour the marinade over the vegetables. Toss and leave for 10 minutes.

Preheat a grill to very hot. Slide the vegetables alternatively onto 8 skewers. Brush with the marinade.

Grill them about 10cm (4 inches) from the heat, turning when required, for about 10 minutes, or until the vegetables are well browned and tender.

Whisk together all the sauce ingredients except for the paprika.

Brush the pita breads with 2 tablespoons olive oil. Heat the breads by wrapping them in a tea towel and placing them in a hot oven.

Remove the skewered vegetables from the grill. Unwrap the stack of breads and place one skewer of vegetables near the bottom of the top flatbread. Pull out the skewer, and place a dollop of sauce on top, followed by a drizzle of marinade and a sprinkle of paprika.

Roll up the souvlaki and secure with a toothpick, or wrap in wax paper. Repeat for the remaining souvlakia.

Serve immediately.

Note: If using wooden skewers, be sure to soak them in water for $\frac{1}{2}$ hour first to avoid them catching fire.

Calzone are popular half-moon shaped stuffed savoury-or-sweet pastries from Italy. This is my version of the savoury variety eaten in the southern region of Campania, Basilicata, and Puglia. Serve calzone as part of a traditional Italian vegetarian meal or as an entree or snack, either hot or cold.

Dough resting time:
1 hour 30 minutes

Preparation & frying time:
about 1 hour 10 minutes

**Makes: about
18 calzone**

Pastry

- 3 teaspoons fresh yeast
- ½ cup warm water
- 1 teaspoon sugar
- 4 cups plain flour
- 1 teaspoon salt
- 3 tablespoons olive oil

Filling

- 1 tablespoon olive oil
- ¼ teaspoon yellow asafetida powder
- 2 tablespoons red or green peppers, finely diced
- ½ cup black olives, chopped
- 1 teaspoon salt
- ¼ teaspoon black pepper
- 2 cups ricotta cheese (or cottage cheese or fresh curd cheese, crumbled)

- ½ cup grated Parmesan cheese
- ⅓ cup grated cheddar cheese,
- ½ cup spinach leaves, chopped and lightly blanched
- ⅓ cup chopped fresh parsley
- oil for deep frying

Ricotta Cheese-filled Pastries

Calzone

Dissolve the yeast in the warm water, add the sugar, mix well, and leave covered in a warm place for 10 minutes or until the mixture froths.

Sift the flour and salt into a large mixing bowl. Add the yeast, oil, and enough lukewarm water to make a smooth dough.

Knead well for 5 minutes. Rub oil inside the bowl and over the dough. Place the dough in the bowl, cover, and let rise in a warm place for 1 hour or until doubled in size.

Prepare the filling

Heat the olive oil in a small frying pan over moderate heat. Sauté the asafetida in the hot oil for a few seconds; then add the diced peppers and sauté for one minute. Add the chopped black olives, salt, and pepper and stir to mix; then remove from the heat and allow to cool.

Combine the ricotta cheese, Parmesan cheese, cheddar cheese, cooled olives and pepper mixture, spinach, and parsley in a large bowl. Mix well and set aside.

Punch down the dough with your fist, remove it from the bowl onto a floured bench top, and knead again for one minute. Roll the dough out with your hands into a long tube and cut into 18 portions. Roll each portion into a smooth ball and, with a rolling pin, roll out each ball into a 13 cm (5-inch) disk.

Divide the filling into 18 portions. Place a portion in the centre of each disk. Fold over and seal around the edge either with a fork or by pressure from your fingertips to make small semicircular pastries. Place all the pastries on a oiled tray and leave them covered with a cloth in a warm place for 30 minutes.

Heat the oil for deep-frying in a wok or large pan over moderate heat (180°C/355°F) and fry 6 pastries, turning when required, until they are golden brown. Remove and drain. Repeat until all the pastries are fried.

Serve calzone either hot, warm, or cold.

I allowed my imagination to run wild when I mentally constructed this multi-layered, deep-dish lasagna before embarking on my test kitchen procedures. You may like to substitute different vegetables in some of the layers. Thin slices of butternut pumpkin can be successfully grilled and added, as can slices of zucchini. Select a casserole dish 25cm x 35cm x 8cm (10 inches x 14 inches x 3½ inches) deep for this "Queen of Lasagna".

Rich & Tasty Lasagna with Grilled Vegetables & Sun-dried Tomatoes

Prepare the tomato sauce

Pour the olive oil into a large, heavy-based saucepan and set it over moderate heat. When the oil is hot, sprinkle in the yellow asafetida powder, fry momentarily, then add the basil leaves and oregano, and fry for another 30 seconds. Pour in the puréed tomatoes, stir to mix and bring to the boil. Add the salt, black pepper, sugar and tomato paste, reduce the heat slightly and cook, uncovered, stirring often for 10-15 minutes, or until it reduces and thickens.

Prepare the bechamel sauce

Melt the butter in a 2-litre/quart heavy saucepan over low heat. Stir in the nutmeg, black pepper and flour, and fry, stirring constantly, for about half a minute or until the mixture

loosens. Remove the saucepan from the heat, and gradually pour in the warm milk, stirring with a whisk until it is all incorporated and the sauce is smooth. Return the sauce to moderate heat and bring to the boil,
stirring. Reduce the heat and simmer for about 5 minutes, stirring constantly, until the sauce develops a thick custard-like consistency.

Assemble the lasagna

Combine all three cheeses (except the reserved Parmesan). Divide the cheese into 2 portions, the tomato sauce into 3 portions, the bechamel sauce into 4 portions, and the pasta into 5.

Spread one portion of the tomato sauce on the bottom of the oven-proof casserole dish. Place a portion of the pasta on top. Layer the eggplant slices on top of the pasta sheets. Spread on a portion of the bechamel sauce, then another of the pasta. Sprinkle on half the grated cheese.

Continue layering as follows: a portion of the tomato sauce; the sun dried tomatoes; the capsicum slices; another portion of the pasta; another of the bechamel; another of the pasta, then the remaining cheese. Layer the spinach leaves on top of the cheese.

Spread on the remaining tomato sauce, top with the last pasta sheets and the remaining double portion of bechamel (this white sauce layer needs to be thicker than the others). Sprinkle the top with the reserved Parmesan cheese, place the lasagna in the top half of a pre-heated 200°C/390°F oven.

Bake for 45-60 minutes, or until the top is slightly golden and the pasta yields easily to a knife point. If the lasagna is darkened on top but does not yield fully to a knife point, cover the lasagna with brown paper or aluminium foil in the last 15 minutes of cooking. When the lasagna is done, leave it in the oven with the door ajar for at least 30 minutes more to allow the lasagna to "plump" up and set. Cut and serve as required.

Preparation & cooking time: approx 1 hour 45 minutes

Makes: 1 deep-dish lasagna

The vegetables

- **1 large eggplant sliced into 0.5cm (¼-inch) rings and grilled**
- **3 large red capsicums (peppers) cut into quarters lengthwise, cored, de-veined and grilled**
- **the leaves from ½ large bunch English spinach, stalks removed**
- **½ cup sun dried tomatoes sliced into strips**

The tomato sauce

- **¼ cup olive oil**
- **½ teaspoon yellow asafetida powder**
- **1 cup fresh basil, chopped**
- **2 teaspoons dried oregano**
- **6 cups tomato purée**
- **1 teaspoon salt**
- **¼ teaspoon black pepper**
- **1 teaspoon raw or brown sugar**
- **2 tablespoons tomato paste**

The bechamel sauce

- **125g (4½ ounces) butter**
- **¼ teaspoon nutmeg powder**
- **¼ teaspoon black pepper**
- **½ cup plain flour**
- **4 cups warmed milk**

The cheeses

- **3½ cups grated cheddar cheese**
- **2 cups grated mozarella cheese**
- **½ cup grated Parmesan cheese plus 3 tablespoons reserved**

The pasta

- **500g (a little over 1 pound) instant lasagna sheets**

Preparation & cooking time:
1½ hours

Pumpkin baking time:
about 1 hour

Serves: 4-6 persons

The dumplings

- **800g (28 ounces)**
  pumpkin, weighed after
  peeling and deseeding

- **a bit less than 1½ cups**
  unbleached plain flour

- **1½ teaspoons salt**

- **½ teaspoon**
  black pepper

The sage butter

- **2½ tablespoons**
  melted butter

- **2 tablespoons chopped**
  fresh sage leaves

- **5 tablespoons**
  Parmesan cheese

nocchi makes a refreshing change to pasta. This recipe hails from the north of Italy where the cuisine displays a distinct Germanic influence. The secret of these little delicacies is to first bake the pumpkin rather than boil it. Because baking vegetables allows them to give off some of their water content, the dumplings need less flour to hold them together, and, along with the caramelised flavours that develop in the baked pumpkin, the gnocchi have a superior flavour. Choose a flavoursome, dry-fleshed butternut or Japanese pumpkin, or your own choice. Avoid watery pumpkins.

Pumpkin Dumplings with Sage-scented Butter

Gnocchi di Zucca

Bake the pumpkin in a hot oven for about 1 hour or until very tender. Remove and mash thoroughly.

Bring to the boil a large saucepan of salted water over full heat.

Melt the butter in another, smaller saucepan. Remove it from the heat and mix in the chopped sage. Set it aside.

Combine the mashed pumpkin with the

flour, salt and pepper. Work the mixture into a paste. It will be a little sticky, but do not add more flour. Form the paste into 40 balls, and divide them between 2 plates. Take 1 plate of balls to the boiling water.

Dip the prongs of a fork in the water and press a ball. It will simultaneously flatten slightly and be marked with ridges. Repeat for all the balls, dipping the fork back into the water between dumplings.

When you've completed pressing the dumplings, transfer half the plate of dumplings, one at a time, with the fork, into the water. They will probably stick to the fork, so submerge the dumpling and the end of the fork momentarily in the water, and the dumpling will slide off. The dumplings will sink, then gradually float to the surface. Make sure the water stays boiling. When the last dumpling has fully risen to the surface, allow them to cook for another 2 minutes, then remove the dumplings from the pan with a slotted spoon and drain them.

Repeat this procedure until the remaining dumplings have been cooked.

Serve hot, drizzled with the warmed, herbed butter and a sprinkling of the grated cheese.

As an alternative serving suggestion, serve Gnocchi di Zucca with a lightly herbed tomato sauce and a topping of Parmesan cheese. You'll need about 2 cups sauce.

Preparation & cooking time:
about 1 hour 35 minutes

Pastry soaking time:
a few hours, or overnight

Makes: 16 pastries

The filling

- ⅔ cup chopped walnuts
- ⅔ cup chopped pistachios
- ⅔ cup chopped blanched almonds
- 1 teaspoon cinnamon
- ¼ teaspoon freshly-grated nutmeg
- ½ cup sugar

The syrup

- 2 cups sugar
- 1½ cups water
- one 10cm (4-inch) cinnamon stick
- 4 whole cloves
- one large strip lemon zest
- 2 teaspoons lemon juice

The pastry

- 250g (9 ounces) unsalted butter
- 500g (little over a pound) kataifi pastry

These aromatic stuffed pastries are a well-known sight in sweet shops throughout Greece, Turkey and the Middle East. Known as kataifi in Greece and kadayif in Turkey, they feature very thin white strands of a vermicelli-like dough that is made by pouring and shaking flour and water batter through a sieve onto a hot metal plate. The raw pastry, also known as kataifi, kadayif or konafa, is available frozen from Greek, Turkish or Middle Eastern stores worldwide, where you will often see the baked pastries arranged for sale on large trays. For best results, pour the hot syrup onto the hot pastries as soon as you remove them from the oven, and serve them the following day.

Greek-style Nut-filled Pastries in Fragrant Syrup

Kataifi

Prepare the filling

Combine all the filling ingredients in a bowl, and mix well. Divide into 8 portions.

Prepare the syrup

Place all the syrup ingredients in a small saucepan over low heat. Stir to dissolve the sugar, increase the heat and bring the syrup to the boil. Reduce the heat, simmer for 10 minutes, then remove the syrup from the heat and set it aside.

Assemble the pastries

Melt the butter. Remove the kadaifi pastry from the packet, and carefully separate it on a flat surface into 8 equal-sized portions, being careful not to smash the delicate strands.

Tease one portion of pastry into a rectangle measuring 15cm x 22.5cm (6 inches x 9 inches). Try to ensure that the strands are all running the same way. Brush the pastry generously with melted butter.

Spoon and spread one portion of filling along the narrow edge of the pastry. Grasp the pastry strands carefully with both hands and carefully and firmly roll the pastry into a tight roll measuring 5cm x 15cm (2 inches x 6 inches).

Repeat for all the remaining portions of pastry and filling.

Pre-heat the oven to 190°C/375°F. Butter a 20cm x 30cm (8 inches x 12 inches) baking dish. Carefully lift the pastries and place them packed closely together in two rows of four. Brush them with any remaining butter.

Bake on one shelf above the centre of the oven for 50-55 minutes, or until the pastries are golden brown. Meanwhile, re-boil the sugar syrup, remove from the heat, and discard the cloves, lemon zest and cinnamon stick.

Pour the hot syrup evenly over the hot pastries. Cover the tray with a tea towel and leave to cool. Cut the pastries once across to form 16 even-sized pieces.

Leave for a few hours, or overnight, at room temperature before serving. The kataifi will be soft and sticky-sweet underneath, but will remain crisp and golden on top.

Popular throughout Italy, especially in the south and Sicily, croccante (literally 'crunchy') is a mixture of caramelised sugar and almonds that are left to harden. It is then broken into pieces for use as a confection or ground up for use as a flavouring. Croccante is fairly simple to prepare, but it must be handled quickly and deftly to avoid the sugar overcooking and becoming bitter, as well as to avoid burns.

Preparation & cooking time:
20 minutes

Makes: 2 cups

- 1 cup sugar
- 1 tablespoon light corn syrup
- 1½ cups whole, blanched almonds, lightly toasted

Sicilian Almond Brittle

Croccante

Combine the sugar and corn syrup in a wide, heavy pan over low heat. Stir continuously with a metal spoon until the mixture looks like wet sand. Allow the mixture to melt and caramelise, stirring occasionally. Meanwhile, have a clean heat proof platter nearby on which to spread the finished brittle.

Remove the pan from the heat when the sugar is a clear, amber colour.

Stir in the almonds quickly, and pour the molten croccante out of the pan onto the waiting platter. Very quickly spread it out with the spoon. Allow the croccante to cool and harden.

Serve Break the croccante into pieces, or use as required.

This is a simple but delectable dessert. Serve warm or at room temperature.

Italian-style Rice Pudding

Bring to the boil 4 litres water in a large saucepan over full heat. Add the rice, return the water to the boil, and boil for 8 minutes. Drain the rice in a strainer, discarding the water.

Heat the milk in another heavy 3-litre/ quart saucepan, preferably non-stick, over fairly high heat, stirring often. When it boils, add the partly-cooked rice, the cinnamon, nutmeg and the orange zest. Return to the boil, then reduce the heat to low.

Simmer, stirring frequently, for 40 minutes or until the dessert reaches a thin pudding consistency. Towards the end you will need to stir the creamed rice dessert constantly to avoid it sticking or scorching.

Add the sugar and set the pudding aside for an hour to cool.

Fold in the ricotta cheese and vanilla extract.

Serve: Spoon the rice pudding into a serving dish and garnish with the reserved almonds.

Preparation and cooking time: about 50 minutes, plus cooling time

Serves: 6-8 persons

- ¾ cup arborio or other Italian superfino rice
- 6 cups fresh whole milk
- ¼ teaspoon cinnamon powder
- ¼ teaspoon freshly grated nutmeg
- 1 teaspoon finely grated orange zest (avoid the white pith)
- ½ cup sugar
- 1 cup fresh ricotta cheese
- 2 teaspoons pure vanilla extract
- 2-3 tablespoons flaked, sliced or slivered almonds

INDIA

South India has many regional varieties of rasam. This one comes from Bangalore. The recipe for home made rasam powder, the main seasoning ingredient in this spicy dal, appears below. Though you can purchase rasam powder at any Asian goods store, home made is preferable.

Preparation & cooking time: 1 hour 10 minutes

Serves: 4 persons

- ½ cup toor dal
- 2 teaspoons fresh hot green chili, minced
- 4 cups water
- 2 ripe tomatoes, finely chopped
- 1 tablespoon chopped fresh coriander leaves
- 1 tablespoon rasam powder (recipe follows)
- 1 teaspoon salt
- ¼ teaspoon sugar
- ½ teaspoon tamarind concentrate
- 1 tablespoon ghee or oil
- 1 teaspoon mustard seeds
- 6 curry leaves
- 1 teaspoon cumin seeds
- ¼ teaspoon yellow asafetida powder
- ¼ teaspoon turmeric

Fiery South Indian Toor Dal Soup

Rasam

Bring to the boil the *toor dal,* water, and chopped green chilies in a heavy saucepan. Reduce the heat and simmer for 45 minutes or until the dal becomes soft.

Add the tomato, chopped fresh coriander, and rasam powder. Continue cooking the soup for another 7-8 minutes, stirring occasionally.

Stir in the salt, sugar, and tamarind concentrate. Continue cooking for another 7-8 minutes.

Heat the ghee or oil in a small pan. When it becomes very hot, add the mustard seeds and sauté them until they crackle and turn grey. Brown the curry leaves and cumin seeds; then add the asafetida and turmeric. Add this hot seasoning mixture to the simmering *dal.* Allow the flavours to mix.

Serve hot with plain rice.

Rasam Powder

1 teaspoon oil
1 teaspoon mustard seeds
½ cup whole coriander seeds
6 whole dried hot red chilies
1 teaspoon black peppercorns
1½ teaspoons fenugreek seeds
2 teaspoons cumin seeds

Heat the oil in a heavy pan over moderate heat.

Fry the mustard seeds in the hot oil until they crackle. Add all other ingredients. Stir well, reduce the heat to medium, and roast all the spices until they turn brown (about 3 minutes), stirring constantly.

Remove the spices from the pan and allow them to cool.

Grind the spices to a powder. This mixture can be stored for some time in a sealed jar.

*B*asmati rice is the famous light-textured, long-grained aromatic rice from North India and Pakistan. It has a wonderful fragrance and flavour, even just served plain. Basmati rice is easy to cook, and although more costly than other long-grained rice, it is well worth the extra expense. This rice dish, studded with crisp toasted cashews, green peas and fresh coriander leaves is an ideal dish to make for a party or a special luncheon.

Basmati Rice with Cashews, Peas & Fresh Coriander

- Preparation & cooking time: 35 minutes
- Serves: 4-6 persons
  - 2¾ cups water
  - 1½ teaspoons salt
  - ½ teaspoon turmeric
  - 2 tablespoons ghee or olive oil
  - ½ teaspoon yellow asafetida powder
  - 1½ cups basmati rice
  - 1 cup peas
  - 1 cup toasted cashews
  - ¼ cup chopped coriander leaves
  - extra coriander leaves for garnish

Bring to a boil the water, salt and turmeric in a small saucepan over moderate heat. Cover tightly and reduce to a simmer.

Heat the ghee or oil in another, larger saucepan over moderate heat. Sprinkle in the yellow asafetida powder, stir briefly, add the rice and lightly fry the grains for about 2 minutes, or until the rice turns a little whitish in colour.

Pour the simmering water into the rice, stir briefly, and if using fresh peas add them now. Increase the heat, return the rice to a full boil, reduce the heat to very low and cover with a tight-fitting lid.

Simmer the rice for 15-20 minutes or until all the water is absorbed and the rice is tender and flaky. If using thawed frozen peas, lift the lid 5 minutes before the end and toss the peas in, quickly replacing the lid.

Remove the saucepan from the heat, leaving it covered and undisturbed for 5 minutes to allow the tender grains to firm up.

Fold in the cashews and chopped coriander leaves.

Serve hot, garnished with the remaining herbs.

Dough resting time:
½-3 hours

Preparation & cooking time:
30-45 minutes

Makes: 12 chapatis

- **2 cups sifted chapati flour**
- **½ teaspoon salt (optional)**
- **water**
- **extra flour for dusting**
- **melted butter or ghee (optional, for spreading over chapatis after they've been cooked)**

*C*hapatis are one of India's most popular breads. They are enjoyed especially in the northern and central regions of India. They are partially cooked on a hot griddle and finished over an open-heat source. Chapatis are made from special whole-meal flour called atta, available from Indian grocers. If unavailable, substitute sifted wholemeal flour. You can spread melted butter or ghee on the chapatis after they are cooked. Chapatis are usually served at lunch or dinner and are great whether served with a 5-course dinner or just with a simple dal and salad.

Griddle-baked Bread

Chapati

Combine the flour and salt in a mixing bowl. Add up to ⅔ cup water, slowly pouring in just enough to form a soft kneadable dough. Turn the dough onto a clean working surface.

Knead the dough for about 8 minutes or until silky-smooth. Cover with an over-turned bowl and leave for ½-3 hours.

Re-knead the dough again for 1 minute. Divide the dough into 1 dozen portions. Roll them into smooth balls and cover with a damp cloth.

Preheat a griddle or non-stick heavy frying pan over moderately low heat for 3-4 minutes. Flatten a ball of dough, dredge it in flour, and carefully roll out the ball into a thin, perfectly even, smooth disk of dough about 15 cm (6 inches) in diameter.

Pick up the *chapati* and carefully slap it between your hands to remove the excess flour. Slip it onto the hot plate, avoiding any wrinkles. Cook for about 1 minute on the first side. The top of the *chapati* should start to show small bubbles. Turn the chapati over with tongs. Cook it until small brown spots appear on the underside (about minute).

Turn on a second burner onto high, pick up the *chapati* with your tongs, and hold it about 5 cm (2 inches) over the flame. It will swell into a puffy balloon. Continue to cook the *chapati* until it is speckled with black flecks. Place the cooked *chapati* in a bowl or basket, cover with a clean tea towel or cloth, and continue cooking the rest of the *chapatis*. When they're all cooked and stacked, you might like to butter them.

Serve *chapatis* hot for best results or cover and keep warm in a preheated warm oven for up to ½ hour.

Dough resting time:
½-3 hours

Preparation & cooking time:
30 minutes

Makes: 16 medium-sized pooris

- **2 cups sifted chapati flour or half-wholemeal and half-unbleached plain flour**
- **½ teaspoon salt**
- **2 tablespoons melted butter or ghee**
- **⅔ cup warm water, or as needed**
- **ghee or oil for deep-frying**

*P*opular over all of India, pooris are ideal to cook for both small dinner parties and festivals with hundreds of guests. On a number of occasions, I've cooked 500 or more pooris in a few hours for big feasts. Once you get the rhythm down, it's effortless and rewarding. Pooris are traditionally made with straight wholemeal flour, but you can vary the ingredients. One-half wholemeal or atta, and one-half unbleached plain flour makes lighter pooris. If you're expert at rolling, try using just plain flour for translucent, gossamer-thin pooris.

Puffed Fried Bread

Poori

Combine the flour and salt in a mixing bowl. Rub in the butter or ghee until the mixture resembles coarse meal. Add up to ⅔ cup water, slowly pouring in just enough to form a medium-soft kneadable dough. Turn the dough onto a clean working surface.

Knead the dough for 5-8 minutes or until silky smooth. Cover with an overturned bowl and leave for ½-3 hours.

Re-knead the dough again for 1 minute. Divide the dough into 16 portions, roll them into smooth balls, and cover them with a damp cloth.

Preheat the ghee or oil in a wok or deep pan over low heat. Meanwhile, with a

rolling pin roll all your balls of dough into smooth disks about 11.5 cm (4½ inches) wide. Increase the ghee or oil temperature until it reaches about 185°C/365°F.

Lift up a rolled *poori* and slip it into the hot oil, making sure it doesn't fold over. It will sink to the bottom then immediately rise to the surface. Hold it under the surface with a slotted spoon until it puffs up into a balloon. After a few seconds, when it is browned to a light-golden colour, turn it over and cook the other side to an even golden colour. Lift out the *poori* with the slotted spoon and carefully drain it in a large colander.

Repeat for all the *pooris*. Serve immediately, if possible, or leave in a preheated, slightly warm oven for up to 2 hours.

This dish originates in Punjab, northern India. However, it is well known all over the world, and there are hundreds of variations of the same dish. But the same main ingredients are always there: peas and panir cheese in a spiced, minted tomato sauce. Here's a delicious version that can be served with any meal, anytime. It especially lends itself to special feasts and dinners and can be kept warm for some time, actually improving the flavour of the dish.

Preparation & cooking time: 45 minutes

Serves: 5 or 6 persons

- 2 tablespoons ghee or oil
- ½ teaspoon black mustard seeds
- 1 tablespoon cumin seeds
- 3 teaspoons minced fresh ginger
- 1 or 2 hot green chilies, minced
- 8 large ripe tomatoes, peeled and diced fine
- 1 tablespoon ground coriander
- 1 teaspoon turmeric
- ½ teaspoon ground fennel seeds
- ½ teaspoon garam masala
- 1 teaspoon brown sugar
- 3 tablespoons chopped fresh coriander leaves or parsley
- 1 tablespoon chopped fresh mint leaves
- homemade curd cheese (panir) made from 2 litres milk, pressed until firm and cut into 1.5cm (½-inch) cubes (see recipe page 51)

Tomatoes, Peas & Home-made Curd Cheese

Matar Panir

- ghee or oil for deep-frying
- 2 cups cooked fresh or frozen peas
- 2 cups whey or water
- 2 tablespoons tomato paste
- 1½ teaspoons salt

Heat 2 tablespoons ghee or oil in a 5-litre/quart saucepan over moderate heat. Fry the mustard seeds until they crackle. Add the cumin seeds and stir until they darken a few shades. Add the ginger and green chilies and sauté momentarily.

Add the chopped tomatoes, powdered spices, sugar, and half the herbs. Partially cover and, stirring occasionally, simmer for about 15 minutes or until the tomatoes break down and turn pulpy.

Heat the ghee or oil for deep frying in a pan or wok over moderately high heat. When hot, (about 185°C/365°F), deep-fry the cubes of *panir* cheese a batch at a time until golden brown. Remove and drain.

Add the peas and water or whey to the tomato and spice mixture. Return to the boil, reduce to a simmer, and cook uncovered for 5 minutes. Add the tomato paste and salt and mix well; then add the *panir* cubes and simmer for 5 more minutes. Before serving, add the remaining herbs.

Serve hot.

Chickpeas are a cousin to the smaller chana dal. They are pale buff to light brown, and look like wrinkled peas. They are used in many Latin American cuisines — Spanish-speaking countries refer to them as garbanzo, and in Italy they are called ceci. They are no less loved in India, where they are a popular choice served in a variety of yogurt or tomato-based savoury sauces. They team up well with many vegetables, such as with tender cauliflower in this classic, succulent and flavoursome Bengali dish. As with all legume dishes, it is appropriate to serve this curry with plain rice, or with a flat bread.

Chickpea & Cauliflower Curry

Chickpea cooking time: about 1 hour

Preparation & cooking time: about 20 minutes

Serves: 4 persons

- ¾ cup dried chickpeas, soaked in cold water for at least 6 hours
- 3-4 tablespoons ghee
- 1 teaspoon turmeric
- 1½ teaspoons salt
- 2½ cups very small cauliflower florets

The paste masala

- one 7.5cm (3-inch) cinnamon stick
- the seeds from 8 cardamom pods
- 1 teaspoon cumin powder
- 1½ teaspoons coriander powder
- ½ teaspoon asafetida powder
- 3 teaspoons very finely minced fresh ginger
- 1½ tablespoons water

Other ingredients

- 1 teaspoon cumin seeds
- 1 large chopped green chili, or more for a hotter dish
- 2 bay leaves
- 2 teaspoons jaggery or brown sugar

Drain the soaked chickpeas, rinse them and transfer them to a 3-litre/quart saucepan with 6 cups fresh unsalted water. Bring to the boil over high heat, reduce to a simmer and cook, covered, until the chickpeas are butter soft. Drain, reserving the cooking liquid.

Grind the cinnamon and whole cardamom to a fine powder in an electric coffee mill or spice grinder. Transfer the powder to a small bowl. Add all the other ingredients for the paste masala and mix to form a wet paste.

Heat the ghee in a 3-litre/quart saucepan over moderate heat. When the ghee is fairly hot, sprinkle in the turmeric and salt, then drop in the cauliflower pieces. Shallow fry the cauliflower pieces, turning often, being careful not to break them, for

3-5 minutes, or until the pieces are just tender. Remove the cauliflower pieces with a slotted spoon and place them in a small bowl.

Stir the cumin, chili and bay leaves into the ghee that remains in the saucepan, and fry until the cumin darkens a few shades. Add the spice paste and fry it for 1 or 2 minutes, or until the ghee oozes out. Add the cooked chickpeas, cauliflower pieces, a few tablespoons of the reserved chickpea cooking liquid, and the jaggery or brown sugar.

Continue to cook over moderate heat, covered, for 3 or 4 minutes more, adding more chickpea liquid if required to keep the dish fairly moist.

Serve hot with rice.

*H*ere's a sample from the wonderful world of potato salads. This recipe is very simply dressed in yogurt and sour cream with a lemon-mustard-mint flavour and a hint of chili.

Preparation, cooking and cooling time: about 45 minutes

Serves: 6 persons

- 8 medium potatoes, unpeeled
- 1 tablespoon fresh lemon juice
- 1½ teaspoons salt
- 2 tablespoons yogurt
- 3 tablespoons sour cream
- ½ teaspoon green chilies, seeded and minced
- 1 tablespoon safflower oil
- 1 teaspoon black mustard seeds
- 2-3 tablespoons chopped fresh mint leaves
- lettuce leaves for serving

North Indian Potato Salad

Cook the potatoes whole in lightly salted boiling water until just soft enough to be easily pierced with a fork. Peel and cut them into 2.5cm (1-inch) cubes.

Combine in a bowl the still-warm potatoes with the lemon juice, salt, yogurt, sour cream, and chilies.

Heat the oil in a small pan over moderate heat and fry the mustard seeds until they crackle. Toss the hot oil and mustard mixture into the salad. Add three-quarters of the mint leaves. Allow the salad to cool for ½ hour.

Serve on a bed of lettuce leaves garnished with the remaining mint leaves.

Karhis are smooth yogurt-based dishes served with rice. Either yogurt or buttermilk is whisked with chickpea flour and then simmered into a creamy sauce. Karhi is an excellent source of vegetarian protein. Yogurt, a complete protein combines with the chickpea flour, an incomplete protein that becomes complete in conjunction with yogurt. Karhi is delicious, light, easy to digest and good for you — what more could you ask!

INDIA

Mixed Vegetables in Creamy Karhi Sauce

Steam all the vegetables until just tender, drain, cover and set aside.

Whisk together the yogurt with the chickpea flour until smooth and creamy. Add the water, chili powder, turmeric powder and coriander powder, and whisk again.

Heat the ghee in a medium-sized saucepan over moderate heat. When the ghee is fairly hot, sprinkle in the mustard seeds, and fry them until they crackle. Add the cumin, fry until it darkens a few shades, then drop in the yellow asafetida powder and fry momentarily.

Pour in the yogurt mixture, and, stirring, bring to the boil. Reduce the heat, and simmer for 10 minutes, stirring occasionally.

Fold in the steamed vegetables, the salt and fresh coriander.

Serve hot with rice.

Preparation & cooking time: 25 minutes

Serves: 6 persons

- 1½ cups carrots, peeled and cut into chunks
- 1½ cups green beans, cut into short lengths
- 1½ cups small cauliflower florets
- 1½ cups green peas
- 2 cups plain yogurt
- ½ cup chickpea flour (besan)
- 600ml (1 pint) water
- 1 teaspoon chili powder
- ½ teaspoon turmeric powder
- 1 teaspoon coriander powder
- 2 tablespoons ghee
- 1 teaspoon brown mustard seeds
- 1½ teaspoons cumin seeds
- 1 teaspoon yellow asafetida powder
- 1½ teaspoons salt
- 2 tablespoons chopped fresh coriander leaves

India   45

*K*hichari (pronounced 'kitch-eri') is such an important dish for vegetarians that I have included a different recipe for it in each of my cookbooks. The flavoursome, juicy stew of mung beans, rice and vegetables is both nutritious and sustaining. It can be served any time a one-pot meal is required. You can practically live on khichari, and in fact some people do. I eat it accompanied by a little yogurt, some whole-wheat toast, lemon or lime wedges and topped with a drizzle of melted ghee. Bliss!

Preparation & cooking time: 40 minutes

Serves: 4-6 persons

- ½ cup split mung beans, washed and drained
- 6 cups water
- 1 bay leaf
- thumb-size chunk ginger, chopped fine
- 1 small green chili, seeded and chopped
- ½ teaspoon turmeric
- 2 teaspoons coriander powder
- 1 cup long-grain rice
- 1 packed cup each broccoli, potato cubes and quartered Brussels sprouts, or vegetables of your choice
- 2 ripe tomatoes, chopped
- 1½ teaspoons salt
- 2 tablespoons ghee
- 2 teaspoons cumin seeds
- small handful curry leaves
- ½ teaspoon yellow asafetida powder
- ½ cup chopped fresh coriander leaves
- wedges of lemon, some chilled yogurt, and extra ghee for serving

Mung Beans, Rice & Vegetables

Khichari

Bring to a boil the mung beans, water, bay leaf, ginger, chili, turmeric and coriander in a saucepan, then reduce to a simmer, and cook, partially covered, for about 15 minutes or until the beans start to break up.

Add the rice, vegetables, tomatoes and salt, increase the heat, and stirring, bring to a boil, then return to a simmer, covered. Stirring occasionally, cook for another 10-15 minutes, or until the rice is soft.

Season: Heat the ghee in a small saucepan over moderate heat. Sprinkle in the cumin seeds, fry until a few shades darker, and add the curry leaves — careful, they crackle. Sprinkle in the yellow asafetida powder, swirl the pan and empty the fried seasonings into the *khichari*. Stir the seasonings through, then return to a simmer and cook for another 5 minutes or so, or until the rice is fully swollen and soft. If you desire a moist *khichari,* add a little boiling water now.

Serve: Fold in the fresh coriander, and serve the *khichari* piping hot with a drizzle of warm ghee, and the accompaniments suggested above.

Koftas are succulent, Indian-style vegetable balls that can be served soaking in sauce or smothered in gravy. A number of vegetables are suitable for making kofta — potato, cabbage, cauliflower, spinach and radish are the most popular. Here are my favourite koftas made from a mixture of cauliflower and cabbage.

Koftas in Tomato Sauce

Preparation & cooking time: 45 minutes

Makes: 24 koftas

Sauce

- 2 tablespoons olive oil
- 1 tablespoon butter
- 2 bay leaves
- ½ teaspoon yellow asafetida powder
- 4 cups tomato purée
- 1 teaspoon dried basil
- 2 teaspoons salt
- ¼ teaspoon freshly ground black pepper
- 1½ teaspoons sugar

Koftas

- 2 cups grated cauliflower
- 2 cups grated cabbage
- 1½ cups chickpea flour
- ½ teaspoon yellow asafetida powder
- 1 teaspoon ground cumin
- 1½ teaspoon salt
- 1 teaspoon garam masala
- ½ teaspoon cayenne
- ghee or oil for deep frying

The sauce

Heat the oil and butter together in a saucepan over moderate heat. When hot, drop in the bay leaves and sauté for 1 minute or until fragrant. Sprinkle in the yellow asafetida powder, and fry momentarily.

Stir in the tomato purée and basil. Raise the heat, bring to the boil, reduce the heat and simmer for 10 minutes or until a little reduced.

Add the salt, pepper and sugar, remove from the heat and keep warm.

The koftas

Combine all the *kofta* ingredients in a bowl until well mixed. Roll the mixture into 24 balls. Heat the ghee or oil for deep-frying in a wok or deep pan, over fairly high heat, to about 180°C/350°F. Carefully drop in 6-8 balls.

Fry the *koftas* for 2-3 minutes or until they rise to the surface and start to colour. Reduce the heat to low, and fry for another 8-10 minutes, or until they are a deep reddish brown. Remove and drain on paper towels. Reheat the oil to its original temperature, and repeat the frying procedure for the remaining batches of *koftas*.

Serve: Soak the *koftas* in the hot sauce 10 minutes before serving time to allow them to fully soak and become plump and succulent. They are great on a bed of steaming hot rice or couscous as part of a main meal. They also work well as an accompaniment.

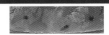

*C*ooked chutneys act as piquant relishes that accent other dishes with which they are served. This North Indian-style tomato chutney is hot, spicy, and sweet. It can be either eaten immediately or refrigerated for up to a week.

Tomato Chutney

Preparation & cooking time: 15-30 minutes

Makes: 2-2½ cups

- 1-2 tablespoons ghee or oil
- ½ teaspoon black mustard seeds
- ½ teaspoon cumin seeds
- one 5cm (2-inch) piece of cinnamon stick
- 3-4 whole dried red chilies, broken
- ½ teaspoon turmeric
- 3½ cups firm, ripe tomatoes, peeled and coarsely chopped
- ⅔ cup sugar
- ½ cup sultanas (optional)
- ½ teaspoon salt

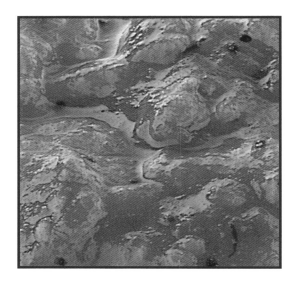

Heat the ghee or oil in a large, heavy frying pan over moderate heat. Sauté the mustard seeds in the hot ghee until they begin to crackle. Add the cumin and cinnamon. When the cinnamon darkens, add the chili bits and the turmeric. Immediately add the chopped tomatoes and, stirring to mix, cook over moderate heat for 10 minutes, or until the tomatoes break down and thicken.

Add the sugar, sultanas, and salt. For moist chutney, continue to cook for another 5 minutes. For a thick jam-like chutney, cook for another 15 minutes or until the chutney appears thick and glazed. Serve warm or cold.

*P*ineapple chutney should be "too hot to bear, but too sweet to resist".

Hot & Sweet Pineapple Chutney

Preparation & cooking time: about 1 hour

Makes: about 2 cups

- 1-2 tablespoons ghee
- 2 teaspoons cumin seeds
- 4 broken dried red chilies, or as desired
- 1 large ripe pineapple, peeled, cored, and cubed
- ½ teaspoon ground cinnamon
- ½ teaspoon ground cloves
- ⅔ cup brown sugar
- ⅓ cup raisins

This is a version of the famous "Radha Red" plum chutney that has been a favourite at many Hare Krishna multi-course feasts throughout the world for decades. It features the subtle and exotic flavour of pure camphor, sometimes available at Chinese and Indian grocery stores. The plums should, if possible, be the Damson variety or the red plums referred to as a "blood plums".

Radha Red Plum Chutney

Heat the butter over low heat in heavy 5-litre/quart saucepan until it froths. Add the coriander, cardamom, and coconut, sauté for one minute, and add the plums. Raise the heat and bring the chutney to a boil; then reduce the heat and simmer covered for about 15 minutes or until the plums lose their shape.

Add the sugar and continue to simmer uncovered for another 40-45 minutes or until the chutney is fairly thick and glazed, stirring occasionally. Add the camphor crystals and mix well.

Serve at room temperature or refrigerate covered for up to 4 days.

Preparation & cooking time: about 1 hour

Makes: about 3 cups

- 1.4 kg (3 pounds) ripe red plums, pitted and cut into eighths
- a pinch of raw camphor crystals
- 2 cups sugar
- 3 tablespoons finely shredded fresh coconut
- 4 tablespoons butter
- 1½ teaspoons ground coriander
- ¼ teaspoon powdered cardamom seeds

Heat the ghee in a 2 litre/quart heavy-based saucepan over moderate heat until it is hot but not smoking. Fry the cumin seeds in the hot ghee until they slightly darken. Add the chilies and cook until golden brown. Add the pineapple pieces, ground cinnamon, and cloves.

Gently boil the chutney, stirring occasionally, over moderate heat for about 45 minutes, or until the pineapple becomes soft and the juice evaporates. Stir constantly as the saucepan dries and the pineapple starts to stick on the bottom.

Add the sugar and raisins and cook for another 10-15 minutes, or until the chutney is thick and jam-like. Remove from the heat and allow the chutney to cool.

Serve at room temperature.

*S*emolina halava is the most popular dessert from the Hare Krishna Restaurant chain worldwide. This version of the famous hot, fluffy pudding with juicy raisins, raw sugar, and walnut pieces rates high in the "halava-top-ten". I have cooked halava for 4 or 5 persons and for 1500 persons; either way, following the same basic steps yields equally stunning results.

Preparation & cooking time: about 30 minutes

Serves: 6-8 persons

- 2¾ cups water
- 1¼ cups raw sugar
- ½ cup raisins
- 140g (5 ounces) unsalted butter
- 1¼ cups coarse-grained semolina
- ⅓ cup walnut pieces

The secret of good halava is to roast the semolina very slowly for at least 20 minutes, with enough butter so as not to scorch the grains. Steam the finished halava over very low heat with a tight-fitting lid for 5 minutes to fully plump the semolina grains; then allow it to sit covered for another 5 minutes. Fluffy, plump grained halava is best served hot, with a spoonful of cream or custard.

Walnut & Raisin Semolina Halava

Combine the water, sugar, and raisins in a 2-litre/quart saucepan. Place over moderate heat, stirring to dissolve the sugar.

Bring to the boil, then cover with a tight-fitting lid and remove from the heat.

Melt the butter in a 2- or 3-litre/quart non-stick saucepan and over fairly low heat without scorching. Add the semolina.

Slowly and rhythmically stir-fry the grains until they darken to a tan colour and become aromatic (about 20 minutes). Add the walnut pieces about half-way through the roasting. Stirring more carefully, raise the heat under the grains.

Turn on the heat under the sugar water and bring it to a rolling boil. Remove the saucepan of semolina and butter from the heat, slowly pouring the hot syrup into the semolina, stirring steadily. The grains may at first splutter, but will quickly cease as the liquid is absorbed.

Return the pan to the stove and stir steadily over low heat until the grains fully absorb the liquid, start to form into a pudding-like consistency, and pull away from the sides of the pan.

Place a tight-fitting lid on the saucepan and cook over the lowest possible heat for 5 minutes. Turn off the heat, allow the *halava* to steam, covered, for an additional 5 minutes.

Serve hot in dessert bowls as it is, or with the toppings suggested above.

Whenever a special festival or feast day comes around, Gulab jamuns are an ideal choice. Guests confronted with them for the first time invariably ask "What are they? " Guesses then range from preserved fruits to doughnuts. In fact, gulab jamuns are made from just milk powder and flour. They're fried slowly in ghee until golden brown and then soaked in rose-scented sugar syrup. Hence, the Hindi words gulab jamun meaning "rose ball".

It is important to note that even though it only takes a few minutes to mix the dough, the gulab jamuns must be fried slowly. If you cook the gulab jamuns too quickly, they will be raw inside. They also must be constantly stirred.

Preparation & cooking time: about 45 minutes

Makes 20 gulab jamuns

- 4 cups water
- 3¾ cups sugar
- 3 tablespoons pure distilled rose water
- ghee for deep-frying
- 6 teaspoons self-raising flour
- 2½ cups full-cream milk powder
- ¾ cup warm milk, or as required

Deep-Fried Milk Fudge Balls in Rose Syrup

Gulab Jamun

Combine the water and sugar in a 3-litre/quart pan over moderate heat and stir constantly until the sugar has dissolved. Raise the heat and boil for 5 minutes. Remove the syrup from the heat. Add the rose water and set aside.

Heat the ghee to a depth of 6.7-7.5 cm (2½-3 inches) in a non-stick deep-frying vessel at least 25 cm (10 inches) in diameter. Place over very low heat.

Make the dough:
Sift the flour and milk powder into a small bowl. Pour the warm milk into a large bowl. Sprinkle the small bowl of milk powder and flour into the large bowl of warm milk while mixing with your other hand. Quickly mix and knead the combination into a moist, smooth, and pliable dough.
Wash your hands, rub a film of warm ghee on them, and divide the dough into 20 portions. Roll those portions into 20 smooth balls. Place them onto an oiled tray or plate.

When the ghee temperature reaches 102°C/216°F, drop the balls in, one by one. The balls will initially sink to the bottom. Do not try to move them. You can, however, gently shake the deep-frying vessel from side to side occasionally until the balls start to rise to the surface. From this point on they must be gently and constantly stirred, rolling them over and over with the back of a slotted spoon, allowing them to brown evenly on all sides.

After 5 minutes, the temperature of the ghee will have increased to about 104°C/220°F and the balls will have started to expand.

After 25 minutes, the ghee temperature should be about 110°C/230°F and the balls should be golden brown. Test one by dropping it into the warm syrup. If it doesn't collapse within a couple of minutes then remove all the balls (3-4 at a time) with the slotted spoon and place them in the syrup. Otherwise, cook the balls for another 5 minutes. When all the gulab jamuns have been placed in the syrup, turn off the heat under the ghee.

Soak the sweets in the syrup for at least 2 hours. Gulab jamuns can be prepared a day in advance, allowing them to fully soak overnight. They can be served at room temperature or slightly warmed.

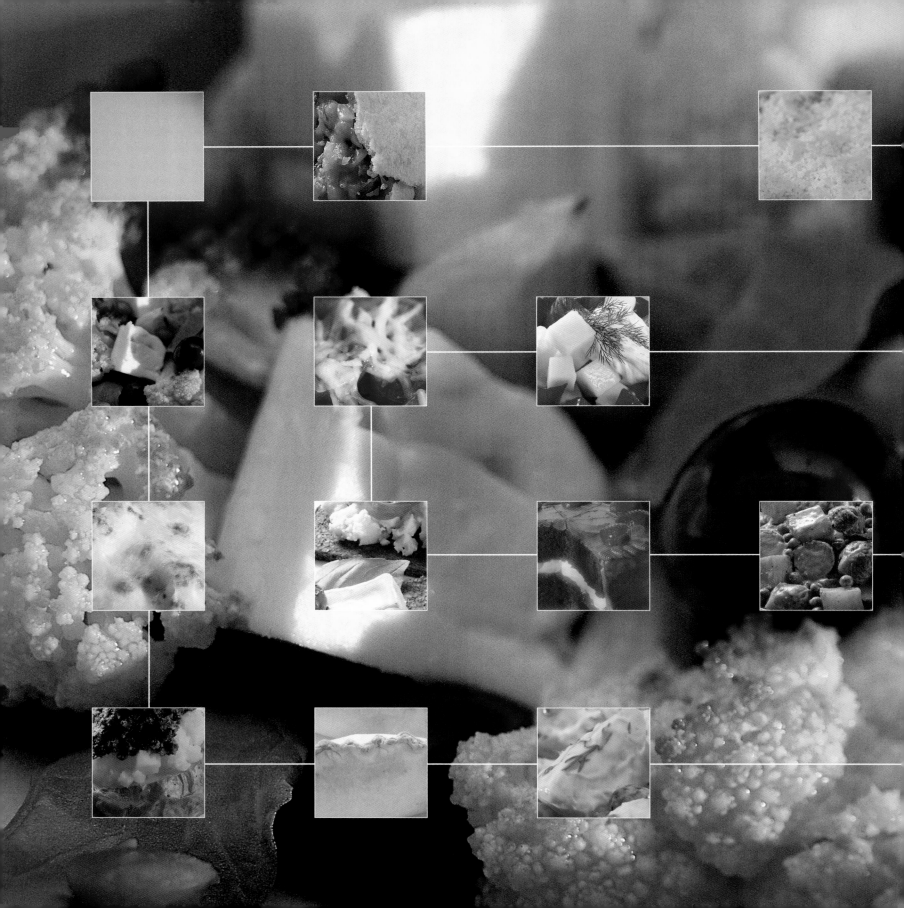

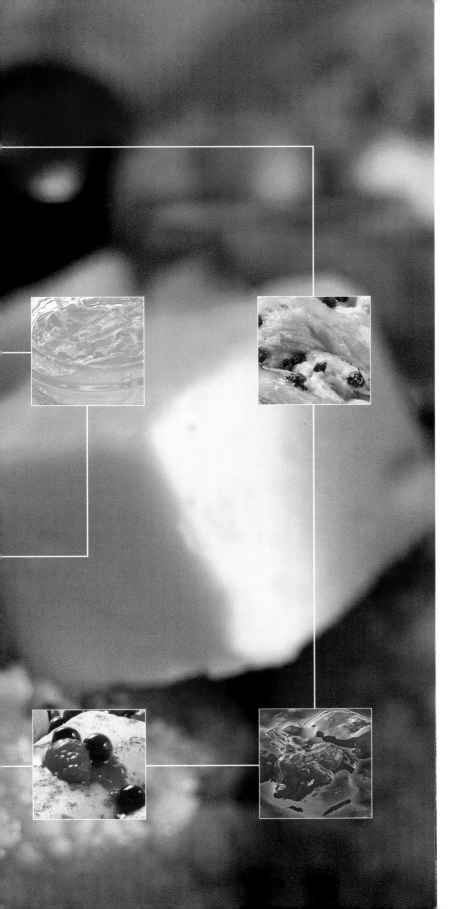

EUROPE

*P*umpkin soup is a great winter favourite. Milk and a simple seasoning of black pepper and nutmeg allow the pumpkin flavour to predominate.

Preparation & cooking time:
30 minutes

Serves: 4 persons

- 3 cups water
- 1½ cups milk
- 90g (3 ounces) butter
- ¼ teaspoon nutmeg
- ¼ teaspoon freshly ground black pepper
- 4 cups, 1 kg (2.2 pounds) pumpkin, peeled, seeded, and cubed
- 1 tablespoon plain flour
- 1 teaspoon salt
- 1 tablespoon light cream
- 2 tablespoons chopped fresh parsley

Old Fashioned Cream of Pumpkin Soup

Melt half the butter in a 6-litre/quart saucepan over moderate heat. Add the nutmeg, black pepper, and pumpkin cubes and sauté for 10 minutes. Add the water and bring to a boil, cooking until the pumpkin is very tender.

Empty the contents of the saucepan into a blender and add half the milk. Purée the mixture carefully. Remove and set aside. Rinse the saucepan.

Heat the remaining butter in the saucepan over moderate heat. Stir the flour into the butter. Return the pumpkin purée to the saucepan along with the remaining milk, stirring constantly until the soup is well blended. Bring to a boil, simmer for a few minutes, and season with salt.

Serve the hot soup in individual pre-warmed soup bowls, garnished with light cream and chopped parsley.

I can still remember the taste of this simple, comforting chunky soup, eaten hot as the cold English rain lashed the window panes. This recipe is almost like my mother used to make — she added eggs to her version of this classic European dish. Mine is much less rich without the eggs, so you need not feel guilty about the sour cream.

Beetroot Soup

Borscht

Preparation & cooking time: about 1 hour 10 minutes

Serves: 6 persons

- 6 medium beetroots, scrubbed and halved
- 2 bay leaves
- 6 cups water
- 1½ teaspoons salt
- 5 old, medium-sized potatoes, peeled and cut into large chunks
- 2 tablespoons fresh lemon juice
- ½ teaspoon black pepper
- 1 tablespoon sugar
- 1 cup sour cream
- fresh dill sprigs for garnish

Simmer the halved beetroots, the bay leaves and the salt in a 5-litre/quart saucepan over full heat covered with the water for one hour or until they are tender.

Boil the potatoes in a separate saucepan in lightly salted water until tender. Remove the potatoes and strain off the liquid. Set the potatoes aside, covered to keep warm.

Remove the beetroots from the water, strain the liquid and reserve it. Rinse the saucepan and return the cooking water to it. Peel the skins off the beetroots under cold running water. Cut the beetroots into large chunks. Return the beetroot to the beetroot water. Add the lemon juice, the remaining salt, pepper and sugar, and place over moderate heat. When the beetroots and their broth are hot, and you are ready to serve, proceed to the next step.

Divide the cooked potatoes between warmed serving bowls. Ladle the beetroot chunks and liquid - as much or as little as you desire - over the potatoes. Dollop with a generous spoon or two of sour cream. Garnish with the dill sprigs and serve immediately.

Sourdough bread is naturally leavened without yeast. Pumpernickel is a richly flavoured, German traditional dark and tasty bread. This recipe is less sweet than commercial pumpernickel and more closely resembles the German black bread, schwartzbrot. Its slow cooking time ensures that it will keep very well. Dense and delicious.

German Sourdough Bread

Pumpernickel

**Dough fermenting time:
16-20 hours**

**Preparation &
baking time: 5-6 hours
(mainly unattended)**

Makes: 1 loaf

- **3 cups coarse rye flour**
- **1¾ cups coarse
  wheat flour**
- **1¼ cups
  coarse barley flour**
- **2 teaspoons salt**
- **½ teaspoon
  powdered fennel seeds**
- **½ teaspoon
  powdered anise seeds**
- **½ teaspoon
  powdered caraway seeds**
- **½ teaspoon powdered
  coriander seeds**
- **2 teaspoons treacle**
- **1 cup plus
  5 tablespoons
  water, heated
  to about
  65°C/150°F**

Combine all the dry ingredients in a large bowl. Dissolve the treacle in the warm water and pour the water into the dry mix to form moist dough.

Knead briefly. Press the dough into an oiled 3-litre/quart capacity rectangular bread-baking tin and flatten the top.

Cover the bread tin with oiled plastic wrap and leave in a warm place (30°C/85°F) for 16-20 hours. If the temperature is right, the dough will naturally ferment and rise in the tin. (The sour fermented aroma is quite natural.) Remove the plastic wrap and replace with a tight covering of foil.

Pre-heat the oven to 107°C/225°F. Fill a large baking pan with boiling water and place at the bottom of the oven. Sit a rack over the pan and place the bread tin on top of the rack.

Bake the bread for 5-6 hours or until it feels firm and looks dark. For the final stage of baking, remove the foil and the baking pan of water from the oven, and increase the oven temperature to 175°C/ 350°F. Bake the bread for another 30-60 minutes or until the top of the bread is crusty.

Remove the loaf, cool on a wire rack and leave 24 hours before cutting into very thin slices. Store in foil or plastic wrap.

 *fabulous, warm short-order winter salad with bold flavours and good looks.*

Oven-roasted Cauliflower, Feta Cheese & Lentils

Preheat the oven to 220°C/425°F.

Combine the cauliflower, light olive oil and salt in a large serving bowl, then transfer to a large deep tray or casserole.

Roast for about 20 minutes or until the cauliflower is slightly golden and cooked al dente.

Return the hot, cooked cauliflower with any pan juices to the serving bowl. Fold the cauliflower with the lentils, feta cheese, olives and watercress.

Whisk together the balsamic vinegar and extra-virgin olive oil and pour over the salad. Gently toss.

Serve immediately, with a grinding of black pepper.

Preparation & cooking time: 30 minutes

Serves: 4-6 persons

- 1 large cauliflower cut into medium florets
- ¼ cup light olive oil
- 1 teaspoon sea salt
- one 400g (14-ounce) can brown lentils, about 1¼ cups, drained
- 250g (9 ounces) feta cheese cut into small cubes
- 1 cup stoned black olives, preferably kalamata
- 50g (2 ounces) watercress leaves
- 1 tablespoon balsamic vinegar
- 2 tablespoons extra-virgin olive oil
- ¼ teaspoon freshly-ground black pepper

With its hot pungent flavour, horseradish is a good counter-part to rich and oily foods, such as this warm potato salad. It's chock full of surprising tastes, colours and textures — aromatic fennel seeds, crunchy smoked almonds, pink-skinned potatoes, fresh dill and lovely green leaves of baby spinach, all coddled in a creamy mayonnaise laced with punch-in-the-nose horseradish.

Preparation & cooking time: 30 minutes

Serves: 6 persons

- 750g (1½ pounds) Pink Eye potatoes cut into large chunks
- 3 teaspoons fennel seeds dry roasted in a pan until aromatic
- ¾ cup chopped smoked almonds
- 3 cups baby spinach leaves, stalks removed

Dressing

- ⅔ cup good eggless mayonnaise
- ⅓ cup sour cream
- 1½ tablespoons fresh dill, chopped
- 1½ teaspoons salt
- 1 teaspoon freshly-cracked black pepper
- 1½ tablespoons grated horseradish, prepared just before adding to the dressing

Warm Potato Salad with Horseradish Mayonnaise

Combine all the dressing ingredients in the bowl set aside to serve the salad.

Boil the potatoes in a large saucepan of lightly salted water until tender. Drain them.

Fold the hot potatoes through the dressing while still hot, and set aside for 10 minutes.

Serve: Fold in the toasted fennel seeds, chopped almonds and baby spinach leaves. Serve immediately.

Rocket, also known as roquette, ruccola, arugula, or rughetta is generally used when the plant is still very young. It appears in the markets with small, slender, multiple-lobed, dark green leaves resembling radish tops, with a peppery, slightly bitter, slightly acidic flavour.

Rocket is one of the many plants that grow wild in the Mediterranean region, and has been used in cooking since Roman times. Today, rocket is one of the ingredients of mesclun, the traditional niçoise mixture of tiny salad leaves. Rocket can also be quickly sautéed in olive oil and served hot with pasta.

Hot Roasted Jacket-baked Potatoes with Arugula Pesto

Bake the potatoes in a hot oven until fully cooked.

Process the rocket leaves and pine nuts in a food processor until the mixture forms a smooth paste. Add three-quarters of the cheese and process some more. With the motor still running, pour in the olive oil until the pesto is smooth and well mixed. Remove the pesto and set it aside.

Remove the hot potatoes from the oven when they are fully cooked, slit them lengthways and fill with generous spoonfuls of pesto.

Serve hot, with sprinklings of the remaining Parmesan cheese.

Preparation & cooking time: about 1 hour

Serves: 4-6 persons

- 6 large baking potatoes, scrubbed and unpeeled
- 125g (4½ ounces) fresh rocket leaves washed, drained and torn
- 2 tablespoons pine nuts
- 1 cup freshly-grated Parmesan cheese
- 3 tablespoons virgin olive oil

I must admit to being very partial to this home-style favourite. Consisting of lightly steamed vegetables in a mornay sauce, topped with grated cheese, and baked in the oven until golden brown, it combines wonderfully with a light soup and bread accompaniment.

Preparation & cooking time:
40 minutes.

Serves: 6-8 persons

- 8 cups assorted vegetables cut into large bite-sized chunks (try a selection from the following: cauliflower, broccoli, carrots, French beans, green peas, baby potatoes, asparagus, squash, pumpkin, sweet potato)
- ⅔ cup butter
- ¼ teaspoon yellow asafetida powder
- ¼ teaspoon nutmeg
- ⅔ cup plain flour
- 5 cups warm milk
- 2 teaspoons salt
- ¾ teaspoon ground white pepper
- 250g (9 ounces) grated cheddar cheese
- 1 tablespoon extra butter
- 2 tablespoons chopped fresh parsley

Vegetables au Gratin

Lightly steam all the vegetables until they're cooked but still a little firm.

Melt the butter in a medium sized saucepan over moderate heat. Remove the pan from the heat. Add the asafetida powder and nutmeg. Stir in the flour with a wooden spoon to make a smooth paste. Gradually add the milk, stirring constantly.

Return the pan to the heat and bring the sauce to a boil, still stirring. Reduce the heat to low and simmer, stirring constantly, for 1 minute or until the sauce is thick and smooth. Add the salt, pepper, and half of the grated cheese. Add the steamed vegetables and mix well.

Spoon the vegetables into a buttered baking dish. Cover them with the remaining grated cheese and dot with little pieces of butter.

Bake in a preheated hot oven (205°C/ 400°F) for 25 minutes or until the top is golden brown.

Garnish with chopped fresh parsley and serve hot.

*B*russels sprouts may not be everyone's favourite vegetable, but believe me, they're delicious combined with golden cubes of deep-fried potatoes, green peas and folded with mildly seasoned sour cream. Serve this tasty and versatile dish as part of a special banquet or dinner menu, with a soup and bread for a warming winter's meal, or with rice.

Brussels Sprouts, Potatoes & Peas with Sour Cream

Preparation & cooking time:
30-40 minutes

Serves: 4-6 persons

- 2 large baking potatoes, peeled and cut into fairly large chunks
- ghee or oil for deep-frying
- 1 cup fresh or frozen green peas
- 2 tablespoons ghee or oil
- small handful fresh curry leaves
- ½ teaspoon yellow asafetida powder
- 2 cups trimmed and halved firm Brussels sprouts
- ¼ teaspoon coarsely ground black pepper
- ½ teaspoon ginger powder
- ½ teaspoon turmeric
- ¼ teaspoon cayenne pepper
- 1-1½ teaspoons salt
- 1 cup sour cream, at room temperature
- 1 tablespoon chopped fresh coriander leaves or parsley

Heat enough ghee or oil in a deep pan or wok that will well cover the quantity of potatoes. When the ghee is hot (190°C/375°F) deep-fry the potato cubes for 8-10 minutes, or until they are lightly golden brown. You may need to fry them in two batches. Remove the potatoes and drain them on paper towels.

Cook the peas in a small saucepan covered with water. Bring to the boil, and cook the peas for 5-8 minutes, or until tender. Drain and set aside, reserving the water. If using frozen peas, boil for 1 minute.

Heat the 2 tablespoons ghee or oil in a 3-litre/quart saucepan over moderate heat. When fairly hot, drop in the curry leaves, and fry them for a few moments. Sprinkle in the yellow asafetida powder, stir

momentarily and then drop in the Brussels sprouts halves. Stir-fry them in the fragrant oil for 3 or 4 minutes. Sprinkle in the black pepper, ginger powder, turmeric, cayenne pepper and salt, stir to mix and add ½ cup water. Stir briefly, place a lid on the saucepan and cook over moderate heat for 10 minutes or until the Brussels sprouts are just tender when stabbed with a knife point.

Add the cooked green peas, fried potatoes, and herbs and then fold in the sour cream. Add a little of the reserved pea water if the dish is a little dry.

Serve immediately.

The Cornish pastie was originally a working man's lunch. The traditional shape had a practical purpose — it was designed to fit into his pocket. Here's a vegetarian version of this English country classic, using minced gluten and vegetables — a hearty lunch for a hard-working vegetarian.

Preparation, cooking & baking time: about 1 hour

Pastry resting time: 30 minutes

Makes: 12 Pasties

The pastry

- 3 cups plain flour
- 1 teaspoon salt
- 185g (7 ounces) softened butter
- ½ cup water
- a little milk for brushing

The filling

- 3 tablespoons butter
- 1 teaspoon yellow asafetida powder
- 1 cup dried soy 'mince' soaked in warm water to plump, then squeezed dry
- 2 tablespoons soy sauce
- 1 carrot, coarsely grated, about ½ cup
- 1 small turnip, coarsely grated, about ¼ cup
- 2 medium-sized potatoes, steamed until just tender, peeled and cut into 0.5cm (¼-inch) cubes
- ½ teaspoon black pepper
- ½ cup chopped parsley leaves

Vegetarian Cornish Pasties

Prepare the pastry:

Sift the flour and salt into a large mixing bowl. Rub in the butter until the mixture resembles coarse meal. Add most of the water, mix well and add the rest of the water if required. Mix well to form a soft dough.

Knead the dough lightly for 2 or 3 minutes, and set it aside, covered, to rest for 30 minutes.

Prepare the filling:

Melt the butter in a heavy frying pan over moderate heat. Sprinkle in the yellow asafetida powder, stir momentarily, then add the soy 'mince'. Increase the heat slightly and stir-fry for about 5 minutes, or until it is lightly browned. Add the soy sauce, stir-fry, then remove the pan from the heat and stir in the carrot, turnip, potatoes, black pepper and parsley. Mix well to combine, transfer to a plate or dish and allow the filling to cool.

Assemble and bake the pasties:

Roll out the pastry thinly on a floured surface, and cut into 12 rounds using a 12.5-15cm (5-6-inch) pastry cutter or saucepan lid. Alternatively, divide the pastry into 12 even-sized lumps, roll them into balls, flatten them into patties and roll them on a floured surface into 12.5-15cm (5-6-inch) discs of pastry.

Pre-heat the oven to 220°C/430°F.

Place approximately ½ cup cold filling across the centre of each disc of pastry. Dampen the edges of the pastry and lift the two sides of the disc, joining them together at the top and pinching together to form a "cock's comb" frill. As an alternative, fold the pastry over in a half circle and seal the edges by pressing them with fork tines.

Arrange the well-sealed pasties, seals upwards, on lightly oiled baking trays.

Brush the pasties with milk.

Bake in the hot oven for 30-40 minutes, or until the pasties are golden brown. Serve warm or at room temperature.

NOTE: As an alternative filling suggestion, add cubes of cooked pumpkin, sweet potatoes, or green peas, or add a few teaspoons of grated cheese.

Knishes are a heavy-duty European Jewish savoury favourite popular in New York. In my version, potatoes are folded with tender vegetables and sour cream and baked in individual flaky pastry cases. Divinely rich already!

Tender Potato Pockets
Knishes

Preparation & cooking time:
about 1 hour 30 minutes

Makes: 10 knishes

The pastry

- 2¼ cups plain flour
- ¾ teaspoon salt
- ¾ cup cold butter
- about 6 tablespoons cold water

The filling

- 2 large whole scrubbed unpeeled potatoes
- 2 tablespoons butter
- 1½ teaspoons ground caraway seeds
- ½ teaspoon yellow asafetida powder
- ½ cup grated cabbage
- ⅓ cup grated carrot
- ⅓ cup finely-chopped green capsicums
- ⅓ cup finely-chopped celery stalks and leaves
- 3 tablespoons minced fresh continental (flat-leaf) parsley
- 1 teaspoon sweet paprika powder
- ½ teaspoon black pepper
- 2 teaspoons salt
- 1 teaspoon sugar
- ⅓ cup sour cream

Prepare the pastry:

Process the flour, salt and butter in a food processor with a metal blade with 12-15 on/off pulses, or until the mixture resembles breadcrumbs. Sprinkle in 4 tablespoons cold water and process again with 6 short pulses.

Add another 2 tablespoons water, and process with another 3 short pulses. Feel the dough. If damp enough to cling together, remove it and form it into a ball and place it onto a lightly floured surface. If a little dry, add a few drops more water. If you are not using the pastry immediately, wrap it in plastic wrap and refrigerate.

Prepare the filling:

Boil the potatoes whole in a large saucepan of lightly salted water. Cook until fork-tender. Drain, peel and mash the potatoes. You should have about 2¾ cups.

Warm the butter in a heavy frying pan or small saucepan over moderate heat. Sprinkle in the ground caraway seeds and the yellow asafetida powder and fry very briefly. Add the cabbage, carrot, capsicum, celery and parsley. Raise the heat and fry the vegetables for 5-7 minutes, or until they are tender. Add the paprika powder, black pepper, sugar and salt, mix well and remove from the heat.

Combine the mashed potatoes, fried vegetables and the sour cream. Set aside to cool.

Assemble and bake the knishes:
Pre-heat the oven to 190°C/375°F.
Form the pastry into a rope and cut
it in half. Roll out half the pastry to
about 0.25cm (⅛-inch) thick on a
floured surface. Cut out 5 discs
of pastry 12.5cm (5 inches) in
diameter. Repeat for the other
half of the pastry.

Divide the cooled filling into 10,
and place a portion of filling in the
centre of each disc of pastry. Gather
the edges of the pastry up over the
filling to enclose it completely. Pinch
the seams together until thoroughly
sealed and smooth to form a sphere
shape, then flatten the spheres
slightly. You may need a few drops
of water to help close the seal.

Bake the sealed *knishes,* seam-side
down, on a lightly buttered baking
sheet for 35-40 minutes, or until
they are golden brown.

Serve warm or at room temperature
with sour cream.

*I*n Switzerland, golden brown flavourful potato pancakes called rosti have been enjoyed for generations. Served plain, these tempting pancakes are a perfect side dish. This version, filled with Gruyere or Emmental cheese and slices of tomato make a delightful breakfast, brunch or light luncheon dish.

Preparation & cooking time: 50 minutes

Makes: 8 rosti

- 8 medium baking potatoes
- ¾ cup olive oil
- 4 tablespoons unsalted butter
- salt and freshly-ground black pepper to taste
- 3 or 4 tomatoes, peeled and thinly sliced
- ⅔ cup grated Swiss cheese

Rosti Pancakes filled with Swiss Cheese & Tomatoes

Boil the whole unpeeled potatoes in a large saucepan of lightly salted water over moderate heat for about 15 minutes, or until a skewer or knife-point easily pierces the outer 1.5cm (½-inch) of potato but meets resistance in the centre. Drain, rinse under cold running water, and if possible refrigerate until well chilled.

Peel the potatoes.

Shred the potatoes lengthwise to form long, even shreds in a food processor fitted with a large shredder blade, or on the large holes of a hand grater. Don't rinse away the starch. Divide the mixture into 8.

Heat 1 tablespoon of olive oil in a heavy 20cm (8-inch) frying pan over high heat until almost smoking.

Sprinkle in one portion of potato into the frying pan. Season lightly with salt and pepper. Quickly push any stray shreds from the outer rim of the pan to form an even, round pancake. Lightly press the top of the rosti. Reduce the heat to moderately high.

Fry the rosti, shaking and rotating the pan occasionally to loosen the potatoes, for about 3 minutes, or until well browned on the bottom. Add a couple of teaspoons of butter to the edge of the pan.

Flip the rosti over, or turn with a wide spatula. Season lightly again with salt and pepper, top with a few slices of tomato, and sprinkle with a couple of tablespoons of Swiss cheese. Continue cooking the rosti over moderately high heat, adding additional butter if the pan becomes dry, for another 3 minutes, or until browned on the second side.

Carefully fold the fully cooked *rosti* in half to enclose the cheese and tomatoes. Keep it warm while you cook the other *rosti*.

Serve the rosti warm or hot.

Rosti Tips

- Shredding the potatoes with a food processor gives the shreds a rounder shape and the pancakes a better texture.

- Be sure to use starchy baking potatoes. The starchiness is needed to bind the shreds of potato.

- Parboil the whole potatoes well ahead of time. Refrigerate for at least several hours before peeling and shredding.

- Add the potatoes when the oil in the pan is very hot and is almost smoking.

- Listen for a soft scraping noise as you shake the pan. When you hear it, you will know the rosti is browned and crisp.

- Cooking two rosti at a time using two frying pans halves the cooking time.

- Rosti may be held for a short while in a warm oven, but they're best served as soon as possible after cooking.

A bittersweet favourite of mine that can be refrigerated for months.

Standing time: overnight

Preparation & cooking time: about 1¼ hours

Makes: about 4 cups

- 3 large ripe limes
- 3 cups water
- about 3½ cups white sugar
- 1½ teaspoons minced fresh ginger

Lime & Ginger Marmalade

Slice the limes into very thin rings and remove the seeds. Combine the limes and water in a bowl and leave to stand overnight.

Heat the lime and water mixture in a non-stick 3-litre/quart saucepan and bring to a boil over high heat. Reduce the heat and simmer, covered, for about 1 hour. By this time the rind should be tender. Remove from the heat.

Pour the mixture into cups and measure exactly how much lime and water there is. Measure an equal quantity of sugar and return the lime and sugar mixture to the saucepan. It is important that you choose the right size saucepan: after you add the sugar to the marmalade, the depth of the sugar, lime, and water mixture should not exceed 5 cm (2 inches), otherwise the jam will be too deep and will not set properly.

Heat the mixture over low heat, stirring to allow the sugar to dissolve. Increase the heat and return the mixture to a boil and cook without stirring for 10-15 minutes or until a spoon of the marmalade sets on a cold plate.

Remove the saucepan from the heat and add the minced ginger. When the marmalade cools, pour it into hot sterilized jam jars and seal the jars.

Try cooking this jam when you have an abundance of ripe, juicy raspberries.

Preparation & cooking time:
15 minutes

Makes: about 4 cups

- 1 kg (2.2 pounds) fresh ripe raspberries
- 4 cups sugar
- 3 cups water
- 1 teaspoon lemon rind, finely grated

Raspberry Jam

Combine all the ingredients in a large heavy non-stick saucepan. At this stage the mixture should be no more than 5 cm (2-inches) deep.

Heat slowly to dissolve the sugar. Increase the heat, bring to a boil, and boil the jam rapidly, uncovered, without stirring for about 15 minutes or until a teaspoon of jam jells on a cold plate. You might have to stir the jam occasionally towards the end.

Pour the jam into hot, sterilized glass jars and seal.

*B*aked desserts look especially attractive when presented in individual ramekins. These little rhubarb crumbles are no exception.

Individual Rhubarb Crumbles

Combine the rhubarb and ½ cup sugar in a saucepan.

Simmer, covered, over moderate heat with whatever water clings to the fruit for about 10 minutes, or until the rhubarb is tender.

Preheat the oven to 190°C/375°F.

Brush 8 ramekin dishes (1-cup capacity) with the softened butter. Divide the rhubarb mixture evenly between the prepared dishes to 2cm (¾-inch) from the top.

Prepare the topping

Place the ginger, baking powder, flour and raw sugar into a mixing bowl. Stir to combine. Rub in the softened butter with your fingers until the mixture resembles coarse bread crumbs.

Spread the topping evenly over each dessert, filling each ramekin to the top. Place the ramekins into a baking tray.

Bake in the preheated oven for 15-20 minutes, or until the juice from the fruit starts to bubble through the crumble topping. Remove from the oven.

Serve each crumble hot or warm with a spoonful of thick cream.

Preparation & cooking time: 30-40 minutes

Serves: 8 persons

Crumble filling

- 1kg (2 pounds) rhubarb stems, washed, trimmed and cut into small pieces
- ½ cup sugar
- 2 tablespoons softened butter for ramekin dishes

Crumble topping

- 1 teaspoon ginger powder
- 1 teaspoon baking powder
- 1½ cups plain flour
- ¾ cup raw sugar
- ¼ cup unsalted butter, softened
- thick cream to serve

This two-tiered carob cake is light in texture without the use of any eggs. The cake's light texture is due to the sour milk. Filled and iced with Carob Vienna Icing, it is an irresistible dessert.

Carob Fudge Cake

Preparation & baking time: about 45 minutes

Makes: 1 two-tiered 20cm (8-inch) carob fudge cake

- 125g (4 ounces) butter, room temperature
- 1 cup caster sugar
- 1 teaspoon vanilla essence
- 1 cup carob powder
- ½ cup hot water
- 2 teaspoons chocolate essence (optional)
- 2 teaspoons fresh lemon juice
- 1 cup milk
- 1⅔ cups plain flour
- 1 teaspoon baking powder
- 1 teaspoon bicarbonate of soda
- pinch salt
- jam and cream to fill
- Carob Vienna Icing (recipe follows)

Preheat the oven to 180°C/355°F.

Cream the butter, sugar, and vanilla until light and fluffy.

Whisk the carob powder into the hot water, add the chocolate essence, and mix to a smooth paste.

Fold together the carob mixture and the butter and sugar mixture.

Combine the lemon juice with the milk to sour it (this is an excellent egg replacement).

Sift the flour, baking powder, bicarbonate of soda, and salt and add it to the creamed mixture alternately with sour milk. Mix thoroughly.

Spoon the cake mixture into two buttered 20cm (8-inch) cake tins.

Bake for 30 minutes or until the tops spring back when lightly pressed. Allow the cakes to cool in their tins for 10 minutes.

Turn out and allow to cool completely. Fill with jam and cream and ice with Carob Vienna Icing.

Carob Vienna Icing

- 125g (4 ounces) butter
- 2½ cups icing sugar
- 4 tablespoons carob powder
- 2 tablespoons hot water
- 1 teaspoon chocolate essence (optional)

Beat the butter until creamy. Sift the sugar. Blend the carob powder with the hot water and chocolate essence. Add the icing sugar to the butter alternately with the carob mixture until it reaches a spreading consistency.

Preparation & cooking time:
1 hour 15 minutes

Makes:
12-14 pancakes

The pancakes

- ¼ cup cultured butter-milk soured at room temperature
- 1 tablespoon sugar
- 2 tablespoons melted butter
- ¼ teaspoon salt
- 1 cup milk
- ¾ cup water
- ¼ teaspoon ground nutmeg
- 1¼ cups self-raising flour

The filling

- 250g (9 ounces) cottage cheese
- 250g (9 ounces) neuf-chatel, or a cream cheese type of your choice
- 2 tablespoons sour cream
- 3-4 tablespoons sugar finely grated outer rind of 2 lemons
- ¼ cup seedless raisins
- ¼ teaspoon cinnamon powder
- ¼ teaspoon nutmeg powder

Blintzes are one of the great specialities of the Jewish Ashkenazic kitchen. Like French crêpes, or Russian blinis, which they resemble, blintzes are thin pancakes that can be wrapped around sweet or savoury fillings, and can play the role of appetiser, main course or dessert. Other sweet fillings could include apple, rhubarb, pears, blueberries or cherries. Potatoes are popular as the basis for vegetarian savoury fillings. Although I use neufchatel, other soft cheeses, such as cottage cheese, curd cheese, cream cheese or quark are all suitable for filling the blintzes.

Sweet, Cheese-filled Pancakes

Blintzes

Pan-frying the blintzes

- 2 teaspoons butter

Toppings or accompaniments

- 2 tablespoons brown sugar mixed with ½ teaspoon cinnamon powder
- or 1 cup berries such as blueberries, raspberries or strawberries or a combination, poached in a little sugar,
- or ½ cup sour cream

Prepare the pancake batter

Combine the buttermilk, sugar, melted butter, salt, milk, water and nutmeg in a food processor. Add 1 cup of the flour. Process until smooth and creamy. Check the consistency of the batter. It should be slightly thicker than pouring cream. Add some of the remaining flour to adjust as required. Pour out the pancake batter and set it aside.

Prepare the filling
Combine all the ingredients for the filling, except the raisins, in a food processor. Process until smooth. Remove, fold in the raisins and set aside.

Cook the pancakes
Heat 1 or 2 shallow, 20cm (8-inch) |non-stick frying pans over moderate heat, until a drop of water sprinkled on bounces off their surface.

Ladle in 3 tablespoons batter, immediately tilting the pan to evenly distribute the mixture to form pancakes to fill the pan. If the batter doesn't spread easily, add a little more water to it. Cook the pancake for 2 or 3 minutes, or until it sets up, the edges begin to curl and the top of the pancake is dry to the touch.

Turn the pancake over, cook for 10 seconds only, then transfer to a plate, undercooked side facing down.

Continue to cook the rest of the pancakes in the same manner, stacking them between layers of non-stick paper. You will probably need to allow the pans to cool between pancakes.

Assemble the blintzes
Heap 2 tablespoons filling on the bottom half of a pancake. Roll up the pancake, tucking in the sides as you go to form a tight rectangular parcel. Repeat for all the *blintzes*.

Melt a teaspoon of butter in a frying pan. Place the *blintzes,* seam down, on the pan. You may need to cook them in two batches.

Fry the parcels over moderate heat until the *blintzes* begin to turn golden brown. Carefully turn them over, and cook for a minute or two on the other side.

Slide the pancakes on to a hot serving plate and serve them with any of the suggested accompaniments.

Preparation & baking time:
about 1 hour 30 minutes

Dough resting time:
about 2¾ hours

Makes: 1 large loaf

- 2 teaspoons
  saffron threads
- ⅓ cup water
- ½ cup butter
- 4-4½ cups unbleached
  plain bread flour
- 1 teaspoon salt
- 1½ teaspoons
  dried yeast
- 1 tablespoon sugar
- 1 cup warm milk
- ¼ cup buttermilk
- 1 teaspoon nutmeg
- 1 teaspoon
  ground caraway seeds
- ½ teaspoon
  cinnamon powder
- ½ teaspoon
  mace powder
- 8 cloves, powdered
- 1⅓ cups currants

For the glaze

- 3 tablespoons sugar
- 2 tablespoons water
- ¼ teaspoon
  lemon juice

*T*inted marigold yellow with saffron threads, this English bread was a favourite for tea in the seventeenth and eighteenth centuries in Cornwall and the south-west of England. In the Victorian period, cooks called it "cake" rather than bread, but it was cooked as bread or buns. It is highly delicious with a prominent heady flavour from the saffron infusion. Note that this bread dries out quite quickly, so eat it fresh, although it can be toasted.

The recipe calls for plaiting of the loaf rather than using a bread tin. Because of the loaf's intricate shape and the fact that it is baked "free-standing", be sure to use a strong bread flour. As far as plaiting is concerned, if you have ever plaited hair, you'll get it first time. If not, try practising with three tightly rolled-up tea towels on the kitchen table. If you can't get it, just make a solid loaf. It will still taste delicious.

Old English Saffron Bread

Carefully grind the saffron threads to a powder in a spice mill or coffee grinder. Place the saffron and water in a small saucepan and heat to barely simmering. Reduce the heat to very low and simmer gently for 15 minutes, or until the water is a rich red colour. Remove the saucepan from the heat. Place the butter in the saucepan and allow it to melt into the saffron infusion. Put the saucepan aside.

Sift the flour and salt into a large bowl. In another large bowl, mix together the warm milk, yeast and sugar. Stir to dissolve the yeast and set it aside in a warm place for 10 minutes or until frothy.

Stir the saffron infusion and butter mixture into the frothy yeast mixture. Add the buttermilk, nutmeg, the ground caraway, cinnamon powder, mace powder and ground cloves. Whisk in 2 cups of the flour and combine until very smooth. Gradually stir in enough of the remaining flour to make a medium-stiff dough.

Knead the dough on a lightly floured surface for about 10 minutes, or until smooth and elastic. Shape the dough into a ball, and place it to rise in a buttered bowl, covered in plastic wrap, in a slightly warm place for 1½ hours, or until doubled in size.

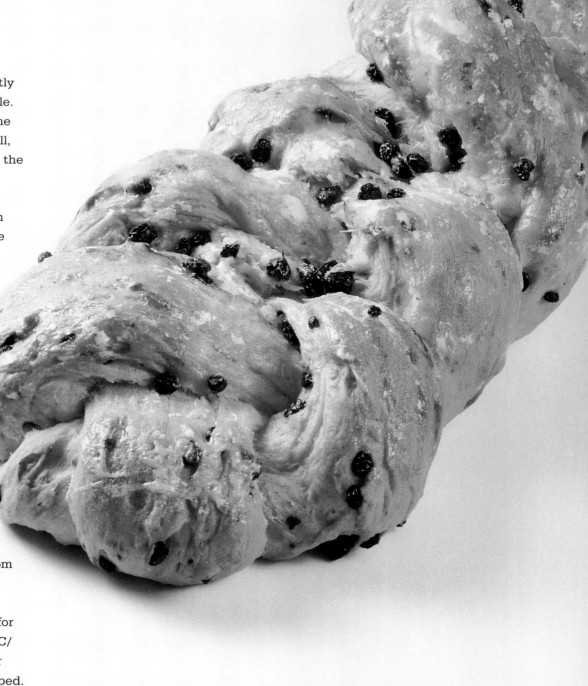

Punch down the dough. Roll it on a lightly floured surface into a 25cm (10-inch) circle. Sprinkle evenly with the currants. Fold the edges in towards the centre to form a ball, working the currants into the dough. Let the dough rest, covered, for 8-10 minutes.

Divide the dough into thirds. Shape each third into a 35cm (14-inch) rope. Place the ropes side by side on a lightly buttered large baking sheet. Beginning at one end, braid the dough, tightly interweaving the pieces without stretching them. Pinch the ends of the strands together and tuck them under.

Leave the loaf to rise again, covered with waxed paper, for one hour or until doubled in size. Pre-heat the oven to 210˚C/410˚F.

Heat the sugar and water together in a small saucepan over moderate heat for the glaze. Boil for 1 minute, remove from the heat and add the lemon juice.

Bake the bread in the centre of the oven for 10 minutes. Then reduce the heat to 195˚C/ 385˚F and bake for another 20 minutes, or until the bottom sounds hollow when tapped. Remove the bread from the baking sheet and place on a wire rack. While the bread is hot, brush it very generously all over with the sugar glaze.

Cool and serve.

THE MIDDLE EAST

*I*n Morocco, Harira features prominently on the menu during the Muslim month of Ramadan, where it is consumed with great gusto every night to break the fast. My vegetarian version is redolent with pepper and saffron, and is made meaty with the addition of chewy chunks of shallow-fried tempe, an easily digestible, high protein soy product. You may prefer to add small chunks of fried panir cheese instead.

Preparation & cooking time: 35-40 minutes

Serves: 6-8 persons

- 3 litres/quarts water
- 1 cup raw brown lentils
- 1 cup cooked chickpeas
- 2 tablespoons olive oil
- 1 teaspoon yellow asafetida powder
- 2½ cups tomato purée
- 250g (9 ounces) tempe, cubed and shallow-fried in hot oil until golden brown
- 1 teaspoon ginger powder
- ½ teaspoon saffron threads, ground and soaked in 2 tablespoons water
- 1 bunch continental parsley
- 1 bunch fresh coriander
- 100g (3½ ounces) wheat vermicelli, broken into small pieces
- 2 teaspoons salt
- 1½ teaspoons black pepper
- juice from 1 large lemon

Moroccan Bean & Vegetable Soup
Harira

Boil the water in a large saucepan over full heat. Add the lentils, reduce the heat and simmer for 10 minutes or until half cooked. Add the cooked chickpeas, and simmer for another 10 minutes or until the lentils are soft but not broken.

Heat the oil in a small pan over moderate heat, and when slightly hot, sprinkle in the yellow asafetida powder. Pour into the soup.

Add the tomato purée, chunks of fried tempe, the ginger, saffron infusion, half the herbs and the vermicelli. Return the soup to a rolling boil and cook the soup for 10 minutes more, or until the noodles are tender. Finally add the salt, pepper, the remaining herbs, and the lemon juice.

Serve hot with rice, couscous, or bread.

NOTE: Instead of adding tempe to the soup, add cubed and pan-fried *panir* cheese made from 2 litres/quarts milk.

I have added chickpeas to this everyday Arab rice dish and transformed it into something very delicious. Served with a crisp green salad and some fresh yogurt, you've made yourself a delicious lunch or dinner. Incidentally, the Lebanese name for this dish translates as "hairy rice", but don't let that put you off.

Arab-style Rice with Vermicelli & Chickpeas

Preparation & cooking time: 30 minutes

Serves: 4-6 persons

- 3 cups water
- 1 teaspoon salt
- 1 tablespoon butter
- 1 tablespoon olive oil
- ¾ cup wheat vermicelli broken into short pieces
- 1 teaspoon yellow asafetida
- 1½ cups long-grain rice, such as basmati
- 1¼ cups cooked chickpeas

Boil the water and salt in a small saucepan over moderate heat. Reduce the heat to low, and cover with a lid.

Heat the butter and oil together in a larger saucepan over moderate heat. When hot, drop in the vermicelli and stir-fry until golden brown. Sprinkle in the yellow asafetida powder, followed by the rice, and sauté the grains for 1 minute or until well-coated in oil.

Pour in the boiling water, allow the rice to come to the boil, reduce the heat to low, cover with a tight-fitting lid and gently simmer, without stirring, for 10 minutes.

Remove the lid briefly after 10 minutes and drop in the cooked chickpeas. Quickly replace the lid and continue cooking the rice for another 10 minutes

or until the grains are soft and fluffy, and all the liquid has been absorbed. Set the rice aside for 5 minutes to firm up. Stir in the chickpeas

Serve hot with a crisp green salad and yogurt.

C hickpeas are a great source of protein and iron as well as fibre, vitamins A and B6, riboflavin, thiamin, niacin, calcium, phosphorus, sodium, and potassium. One cup of chickpeas has the usable protein equivalent of one 30g (4¼-ounce) steak. When chickpeas are combined with dairy products, the useable protein increases.

This famous chickpea pâte is very tasty and goes well as a dip or spread on bread or crackers.

Chickpea Pâte

Hoummos

Preparation & cooking time: about 20 minutes

Makes: about 1¼ cups

- 1¼ cup cooked chickpeas
- ½ cup tahini
- 2 tablespoons fresh lemon juice
- ¼ teaspoon yellow asafetida powder
- a little water
- salt and pepper according to taste
- 1 tablespoon olive oil for garnish
- ¼ teaspoon paprika for garnish
- 1 teaspoon chopped parsley for garnish

Process the chickpeas, tahini, lemon juice, and yellow asafetida powder in a food processor until smooth, adding a little water if required for a puree consistency. Transfer to a serving bowl.
Season to taste.
Serve at room temperature garnished with olive oil, paprika and parsley accompanied by chunks of toasted focaccia.

This Lebanese salad is probably the most famous of all Middle Eastern mezze (hors d'oeuvres). Bulgur wheat (parched, ground, par-boiled wheat grains) is not only tasty and substantial but also very nutritious. It is rich in protein, calcium, phosphorus, iron, potassium, niacin, and vitamins B1 and B2. Bulgur wheat salad is easy to prepare and is characterised by its fresh lemon-mint-parsley flavour. Traditional Middle Eastern cooks sometimes use an extra ingredient in their salads: a tart seasoning made from the ground seeds of a Mediterranean flowering plant called sumac, which adds a special lemony taste. I have included this as optional. It is available from any well-stocked Middle Eastern grocer, as is the bulgur wheat which, incidentally, is sometimes referred to as bourghul or cracked wheat. Tabbouleh is traditionally served in fresh, crisp lettuce leaves. Add more lemon juice if necessary, to assure the authentic fresh-lemon taste.

Lebanese Bulgur-Wheat Salad

Wheat soaking time:
1½ hours

Preparation time:
10 minutes

Serves: 6 persons

- 250g (9 ounces) fine bulgur wheat
- ½ teaspoon yellow asafetida powder
- at least ½ cup fresh lemon juice
- ½ cup olive oil
- 1½ teaspoons salt
- ¼ teaspoon coarsely ground black pepper
- 3 cups finely chopped parsley
- 3 tablespoons fresh mint
- 2 teaspoons sumac (optional)
- 1 cup seeded, unpeeled cucumber, diced into 1.25 cm (½-inch) cubes
- 2 medium tomatoes, diced
- lettuce leaves for decoration

Soak the bulgur wheat for 1½ hours in warm water. Drain it and squeeze out the moisture. Dry it further by spreading it on a cloth and patting it dry.

Combine the soaked wheat, asafetida, lemon juice, olive oil, salt, pepper, parsley, mint, and sumac in a large bowl and mix well. Add the cucumber and tomatoes and toss. Chill and serve with lettuce leaves.

THE MIDDLE EAST

*F*alafel are spicy chickpea croquettes. The original Egyptian variety contained dried white broad beans and were called ta'amia. In Israel, chickpeas were substituted for the broad beans. Falafel are delicious served stuffed inside split Middle Eastern flatbreads dressed with tahini sauce or hoummos and accompanied by green salad.

Chickpea soaking time:
overnight

Mixture resting time:
30 minutes

Preparation & cooking time:
about 30 minutes

Makes: 14-16 falafel

- 1¼ cups chickpeas, soaked overnight and drained
- ½ teaspoon yellow asafetida powder
- ¾ cup finely chopped parsley
- 1 teaspoon ground coriander
- 1 teaspoon ground cumin
- ¼ teaspoon cayenne pepper
- 1½ teaspoons salt
- ¼ teaspoon freshly ground black pepper
- ½ teaspoon baking powder
- oil for deep-frying

Israeli Chickpea Croquettes
Falafel

Process the chickpeas in a food processor and mince finely. Scrape the minced chickpeas into a bowl. Fold in the herbs, spices, salt, and baking powder. Mix well, knead, and leave for 30 minutes.

Form the mixture into 14 to 16 falafel balls. If they're too sticky, roll the falafel in a little flour. Repeat until all the mixture is rolled.

Heat a heavy pan or wok with ghee or oil to a depth of 6.5-7.5 cm (2½-3 inches), until moderately hot 180°C/355°F. Deep-fry 6 to 8 falafels at a time, turning when required, for 5 or 6 minutes, or until they're evenly golden brown.

Remove and drain on paper towels. Cook all the falafel. Serve hot, as recommended above.

There are many versions of this stuffed appetizer, found in Armenia, Turkey, Greece, and the Middle East. A dolma is actually any dish prepared by stuffing a vine, fig, cabbage, or other edible leaf with a savoury filling. Here is a Greek version of vine leaves stuffed with rice, pine nuts, and currants and flavoured with dill and oregano. They can be served cold as an appetizer with salad, bread, and dips or heated in the oven with tomato sauce.

Preparation & cooking time: about 2 hours

Makes: 30-40 dolmades

- 2 cups boiling water
- 2 tablespoons olive oil
- ⅓ cup pine nuts
- ¾ teaspoon yellow asafetida powder
- 1 cup long-grain rice
- ⅓ cup currants
- 1½ teaspoons dried oregano
- 1 teaspoon dried dill
- 1 teaspoon salt
- ¼ teaspoon freshly-ground black pepper
- 1 tablespoon tomato paste
- 2 x 250g (9-ounce) packets of vine leaves
- juice of 2 lemons

Stuffed Vine Leaves

Bring the water slowly to the boil in a covered saucepan over low heat.

Heat the olive oil in a non-stick 2-litre/quart pot over moderate heat. Stir-fry the pine nuts in the hot oil until they turn light golden brown. Sprinkle in the asafetida, fry momentarily then add the rice and stir-fry for 2 minutes. Add the boiling water, the currants, oregano, dill, salt, and pepper. Allow the rice to return to the boil, then reduce the heat to low, and simmer, covered, for 20 minutes.

Remove the rice from the heat and set aside for five minutes for the grains to firm up.

Stir in the tomato paste. Empty the rice into a bowl and allow to cool.

Place the vine leaves in a bowl and scald them with boiling water. Leave them to soak for 10 minutes; then drain and rinse under cold water.

Open up each leaf, placing between 1 teaspoon and 1 tablespoon of the filling (depending on the size of the leaf) rolled into a short tubular shape, into the centre of each leaf. Roll up the leaf, tucking in the sides as you go.

Layer some damaged or unused leaves on the bottom of a large, heavy pot and layer the stuffed leaves on top. If you have more than one layer, place some leaves in between.

Place an inverted plate or saucer on top of the stuffed leaves, add enough hot water just to cover them, add the lemon juice, and cover the pot.

Simmer for one hour over low heat. After they are cooked, allow them to cool in the pot and carefully remove them. Serve the dolmades warm or at room temperature.

*T*ender chickpeas and buttery spinach folded through aromatic tomato sauce appear on many a Middle Eastern dinner table. This sensational Saudi version is flavoured with a popular spice blend called baharat, a generic blend of herbs and spices that varies according to the taste of the spice merchant. My favourite combination is pepper, cumin, coriander, cinnamon, cloves, cardamom, paprika and nutmeg. Baharat is available at Middle Eastern grocers. It is added towards the end of the cooking, much like garam masala in Indian cuisine.

Saudi Spinach with Chickpeas

Heat the ghee or oil in a medium saucepan over moderate heat. Sprinkle in the yellow asafetida powder and fry momentarily.

Pour in the tomato purée, and cook, stirring occasionally, for about 2-3 minutes or until slightly reduced.

Fold the cooked chickpeas into the tomato purée, along with the blanched spinach, the salt, pepper, sugar and *baharat*.

Reduce the heat and cook for an extra 2-3 minutes.

Serve hot, garnished with drizzles of the remaining ghee or olive oil, lemon juice and a sprinkle of fresh parsley, accompanied by thirsty flatbreads to mop up the fragrant juices.

- Preparation & cooking time: 30 minutes
- Serves: 4 persons
- 3 tablespoons ghee or olive oil
- 1 teaspoon yellow asafetida powder
- 1 cup tomato purée
- 375g (13 ounces) cooked chickpeas, about 3 cups
- 450g (1 pound) spinach, leaves, steamed, blanched and chopped
- 1 teaspoon salt
- ½ teaspoon freshly-cracked black pepper
- 1 teaspoon brown sugar
- 1 teaspoon baharat
- extra 2 tablespoons ghee olive oil for garnish
- 1 tablespoon fresh lemon juice for garnish
- 2 or 3 tablespoons freshly chopped parsley for garnish

*C*ouscous, the famous grain product of North African fame, makes a great salad base. Teamed up with a selection of vegetables, tender chickpeas, crunchy peanuts and a mint-parsley, tahini-laced dressing, it is a substantial addition to a summer menu.

Preparation & cooking time: about 15 minutes

Serves: 6 persons

The dressing

- 4 tablespoons lemon juice
- 2 tablespoons olive oil
- 2 teaspoons sugar
- 3 tablespoons tahini
- 4 tablespoons fresh mint leaves, chopped
- 1½ teaspoons salt
- 1 teaspoon freshly-ground black pepper
- ½ teaspoon yellow asafetida powder
- 4 tablespoons fresh parsley, chopped

Couscous Salad

The remaining ingredients

- ⅓ cup tomato, diced small
- ¼ cup red capsicum, diced small
- ¼ cup green capsicum, diced small
- ¼ cup green beans, cut into small lengths and steamed
- ½ cup cooked chickpeas
- ½ cup unpeeled, diced Lebanese-style cucumbers
- ½ cup sultanas
- ¼ cup chopped green olives
- ¼ cup small, roasted peanut halves

The couscous

- 1½ cups water
- 1½ teaspoons salt
- 1½ tablespoons olive oil
- 1½ cups couscous

Prepare the couscous: Bring to the boil the water, salt and olive oil in a small saucepan. Remove the saucepan from the heat, stir in the couscous grains and set the saucepan aside, covered, for 10 minutes. Fluff the grains with a fork, and transfer the cooked couscous to a serving bowl. Allow to cool thoroughly.

Whisk together the dressing ingredients in a small bowl.

Mix the remaining ingredients with the cooled couscous. Add the dressing, mix well and serve immediately.

This crisp, tossed salad from North Africa is a blend of lettuce, tomatoes, cucumbers, radishes, green peppers, parsley, lemon juice, oil, and mint. Serve with flat bread and yogurt for a Middle Eastern feast!

Tunisian Vegetable Salad

Toss the lettuce, tomatoes, cucumber, radishes, pepper, green chili, shredded lettuce strips, and parsley in a large salad bowl.

Blend the olive oil, lemon juice, asafetida, salt, pepper, and mint in a small bowl.

Pour the dressing over the salad when ready to serve, and toss gently to coat. Serve immediately.

Preparation time:
15 minutes

Serves: 6-8 persons

- 1 medium Cos lettuce, torn into bite-sized pieces
- 3 small, firm tomatoes, cut into wedges
- 1 medium continental cucumber, sliced
- 6 small radishes, sliced into thin rings
- 1 small green pepper cored, seeded, and thinly sliced
- 1 small fresh green chili, seeded and sliced into wafer-thin strips
- 2 or 3 inner leaves of Iceberg lettuce rolled up and shredded into wafer-thin strips
- ½ cup chopped fresh parsley, packed
- 4 tablespoons olive oil
- 4 tablespoons fresh lemon juice
- ¼ teaspoon yellow asafetida powder
- 1 teaspoon salt
- ½ teaspoon freshly ground black pepper
- 1 teaspoon dried mint leaves

*F*attoush, a mouth-watering salad from ancient times, incorporates a resourceful way of using up stale Arab flat breads. Fattoush literally means 'wet bread', and traditionally the bread was soaked in water then toasted to revive it. My version of this recipe omits the soaking.

Lebanese Toasted Bread Salad

Fattoush

Preparation & cooking time: 35 minutes

Serves: 6 persons

- 2 medium pita breads
- 1 small romaine or cos lettuce
- 8 pink radishes, quartered lengthwise
- 2 Lebanese cucumbers, peeled and sliced
- 4 large brine-pickled cucumbers, sliced
- 3 medium tomatoes, cut into eighths
- ½ cup finely-chopped, flat-leaf parsley
- ⅓ cup finely-chopped, fragrant mint leaves
- ¼ cup finely-shredded heart of iceberg lettuce
- 1 green chili, seeded and sliced fine julienne

Garnish

- ½ teaspoon freshly-ground black pepper
- 2 tablespoons coarsely ground sumac

Split each of the pita breads in half horizontally so that you have 4 thin rounds of bread.

Toast the breads lightly under a grill until just pale golden and crisp. Break up the toasted bread into small pieces and put in the bottom of a large salad bowl. **Pile** the cut vegetables and herbs on top of the toasted bread.

Whisk together the dressing ingredients, and pour over the salad. Sprinkle with the pepper and sumac, and quickly toss the salad.

Serve immediately so the bread stays crisp.

Dressing

- ¼ cup fresh lemon juice
- ¼ cup extra-virgin olive oil
- 1 teaspoon yellow asafetida powder
- 1 teaspoon salt

A KEY INGREDIENT in fattoush is sumac, a dark red, lemony astringent flavouring much used in Middle Eastern cuisine. Sumac is made from the dried red berries of the bush Rhus coriara, and is available in Middle Eastern shops.

Note that you can use fresh or frozen and thawed Arab bread for this recipe. Traditional versions of this recipe use melokhia leaves, which are hard to come by. I have replaced them with romaine or cos lettuce.

Preparation & cooking time:
30 minutes

Serves: 4 persons

- 2½ cups water
- 1 teaspoon salt
- ¼ teaspoon saffron threads, ground
- 4 tablespoons ghee or clarified butter
- 4 green cardamom pods
- 4 whole cloves
- ½ teaspoon cumin seeds
- ¼ teaspoon black cumin seeds
- ¼ teaspoon fennel seeds
- one 5cm (2-inch) piece cassia bark or cinnamon stick
- 1½ cups basmati rice

*T*he Iranian dish pollou or pillau (from pollo, rice) is a tasty combination of the famous long, narrow-grained fragrant basmati rice cooked by absorption with spices and clarified butter or ghee. This dish was taken to India, where it became pullao, one of the most important rice dishes of the sub-continent. Westwards, this renowned Persian dish became the basis of pilav or pilaf in Turkey and Armenia, the pilafi dishes of Greece and the paellas of Spain.

Iranian Spicy Rice with Saffron

Pollou

Bring to a boil the water, salt and saffron in a saucepan with a tight-fitting lid, and reduce to a simmer.

Heat the ghee in another, larger saucepan over moderate heat.

Stir in the cardamom pods, cloves, the two varieties of cumin, the fennel and cassia, and fry the spices for a couple of minutes, or until they darken a few shades and become aromatic.

Add the rice, and gently stir-fry it for two minutes, or until the grains turn a little whitish in colour.

Pour the simmering water into the toasted grains, increase the heat, and bring to the boil. Reduce the heat to low, cover with a tight-fitting lid and gently simmer, without stirring or lifting the lid, for 20 minutes, or until the water is fully absorbed and the rice is tender.

Remove the rice from the heat, and let it sit, covered, for another 5 minutes to allow the fragile grains to firm up.

Serve piping hot.

Pine nuts are the kernels or seeds that are shed as the pine cones dry, open out and mature in the summer months. These little cream-coloured nuts can be toasted lightly in a dry frying pan, or with a little olive oil, to release a deeper nuttier flavour. Coupled with flavoursome cloves, orange, ginger, thyme, and succulent currants, they add a tasty crunch to this exotic rice dish from Turkey.

Preparation and cooking time: 40 minutes

Serves: 6 persons

- 3 cups vegetable stock or water
- 3 tablespoons extra virgin olive oil
- ½ cup pine nuts
- ½ teaspoon yellow asafetida powder
- 1½ cups basmati rice or other good quality long-grain white rice
- 4 whole cloves
- one 2.5cm (1-inch) cube ginger, sliced
- 2 bay leaves
- 2 whole 10cm (4-inch) stalks fresh thyme
- three 3-inch strips orange zest
- 1½ teaspoons salt
- ½ teaspoon freshly-ground black pepper
- ⅓ cup currants
- 3 tablespoons chopped continental (flat-leaf) parsley

Turkish Pilaf with Currants & Pine Nuts

Bring to the boil the vegetable stock in a small saucepan over moderate heat, cover and reduce to a simmer.

Heat the olive oil in a 2-litre/quart saucepan over low to moderate heat. When slightly hot, add the pine nuts. Toast them in the oil for 1 or 2 minutes, or until they turn light golden brown and smell fragrant. Remove the saucepan from the heat, quickly remove the nuts from the oil with a slotted spoon and drain them on paper towels.
Return the pan and the remaining oil to the heat.

Sprinkle the yellow asafetida powder into the hot oil. Stir momentarily, drop in the rice, and stir-fry it in the oil for 2 or 3 minutes or until the rice grains become a little whitish in colour.

Pour the boiling stock into the rice. Add the cloves, ginger, bay leaves, thyme stalks, orange zest, salt and pepper. Raise the heat to high and quickly bring the rice to a full boil. Immediately reduce the heat to very low, cover with a tight-fitting lid.

Gently simmer the rice, without stirring, for 20-25 minutes or until the liquid is fully absorbed and the rice is tender and fluffy.

Remove the saucepan from the heat, allowing the delicate rice grains to firm up for 5 minutes. Lift the lid and carefully extract the cloves, thyme stalks, ginger and bay leaves which should be sitting on the very surface of the rice.

Carefully fold in the currants, nuts and continental parsley and serve the rice hot.

Wholesome Brown Lentil & Vegetable Soup

Rinse the lentils under cold running water, then place them with about 6 cups water in a 3-litre/quart saucepan over moderate heat.

Bring to the boil, reduce heat to a simmer. Cook for 15-20 minutes or until the lentils start to break up.

Warm the oil in another small saucepan over moderate heat. When warm, sprinkle in the yellow asafetida powder. Drop in the potatoes and black pepper, increase the heat and fry the potatoes for 2 or 3 minutes. Add the celery and fry for 1 more minute. Pour the vegetables and flavoured oil into the simmering soup.

Cook the soup for another 15 minutes, or until the potatoes begin to soften. Then add the spinach leaves, the ground coriander, cumin and lemon juice. Allow the soup to cook for another 10 minutes, or until the vegetables and lentils are all sufficiently tender. Finally add the parsley, coriander leaves and salt.

Serve the soup hot.

Preparation & cooking time: about 45 - 50 minutes

Serves: 4-6 persons

- 1 cup brown lentils
- 3 tablespoons olive oil
- ½ teaspoon yellow asafetida powder
- 1 cup potatoes, diced
- ½ teaspoon freshly-ground black pepper
- 1 cup chopped celery, including leaves
- 1 cup chopped spinach leaves
- 1 tablespoon ground coriander powder
- ½ teaspoon cumin powder
- 2 tablespoons lemon juice
- ¼ cup chopped parsley leaves
- ¼ cup chopped coriander leaves
- 1½ teaspoons salt

*H*ere the exotic muhammara paste is served with grilled ciabatta (the oval Italian bread named after a slipper) along with bite-sized blanched vegetables (crudités) of your choice — great for a picnic or an alfresco lunch.

Preparation & cooking time:
25 minutes

Makes: 1½ cups paste

- 2 large red capsicums (peppers)
- 1 small hot red chili, seeded and chopped
- 1 slice wholemeal bread, crusts removed
- 1 cup shelled walnuts
- ½ teaspoon yellow asafetida powder
- 1½ tablespoons pomegranate molasses
- juice of ½ lemon
- ½ teaspoon sugar
- ½ teaspoon salt
- 3 tablespoons extra virgin olive oil
- 1 tablespoon flat-leaf parsley
- toasted ciabatta bread, to serve
- vegetable crudites, to serve

Syrian Roast Pepper & Walnut Paste

Muhammara

Roast the capsicums under a grill for 15 minutes, or until the skin is blistered and blackened. Place in a plastic bag, seal and set aside for 5 minutes before peeling. Alternatively, grill the capsicums in the coals of a barbecue.

Combine all the ingredients except the parsley, ciabatta and *crudités* in a food processor and blend to a thick creamy paste.

Serve sprinkled with the parsley, and accompanied with chunks of toasted ciabatta and the vegetable *crudités*.

Muhammara Paste

There are many versions of the delicious paste known as muhammara all over the Middle East; this one is from Syria. The sourness of muhammara comes from pomegranate concentrate, sometimes called pomegranate molasses — thick, sour and fruity syrup available in bottles or jars from Middle Eastern grocers. The sweet and sour, nutty paste couples well with bread or lightly blanched vegetables.

*B*aklava is probably one of the best known of all Middle Eastern sweets. In this delightful version of Turkish origin, sheets of buttered wafer-thin filo pastry are layered with nuts and baked; then they're soaked in a lemon and orange-blossom flavoured sugar and honey syrup.

Turkish Nut Pastries in Syrup

Baklava

Butter a 28cm x 18cm (11-inch x 7-inch) tin. If necessary, cut the pastry the size of the tin.

Place one sheet of pastry on the bottom of the tin and butter it with a pastry brush. Repeat for half the pastry (about 15 sheets).

Combine the nuts, cinnamon, and sugar.

Sprinkle the mixture evenly over the top layer of the buttered filo pastry. Continue layering the remaining pastry on top of the nut mixture, again brushing each layer of pastry with melted butter. After the final layer of pastry is placed on top, brush it with butter.

Carefully cut the tray of pastry into diagonal diamond shapes with a sharp knife, cutting directly to the base.

Bake in a moderate oven 180°C/355°F for about 45 minutes or until the top is crisp and golden.

Combine the sugar, water, and lemon juice in a pan, stir over low heat to dissolve the sugar, and then boil for 5 minutes. Remove from the heat, add the honey, stir to dissolve, and add the orange-blossom water.

Pour the hot syrup over the cooked baklava. Let set for at least 2 hours, or for best results leave overnight for the syrup to be fully absorbed before serving.

Preparation & cooking time: about 1 hour 5 minutes

Baklava soaking time: overnight, or at least 2 hours

Makes: about 18 large pieces

Pastries

- 450g (1 pound) filo pastry (about 30 sheets)
- 250g (9 ounces) unsalted butter, melted
- 250g (9 ounces) finely chopped walnuts (or almonds, pistachios, or a combination)
- 1 teaspoon cinnamon powder
- ¼ cup sugar

Syrup

- 1¼ cups sugar
- 1 cups water
- 2 tablespoons lemon juice
- ¼ cup honey
- 1 tablespoon orange-blossom water (available at Middle Eastern grocers)

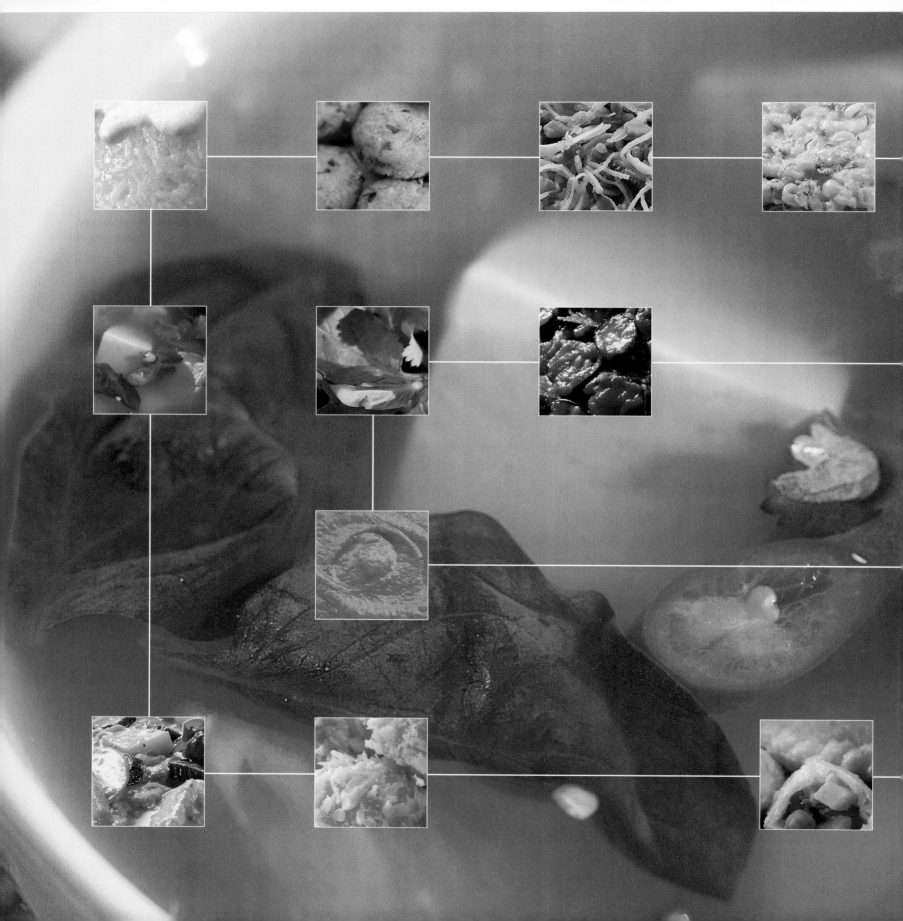

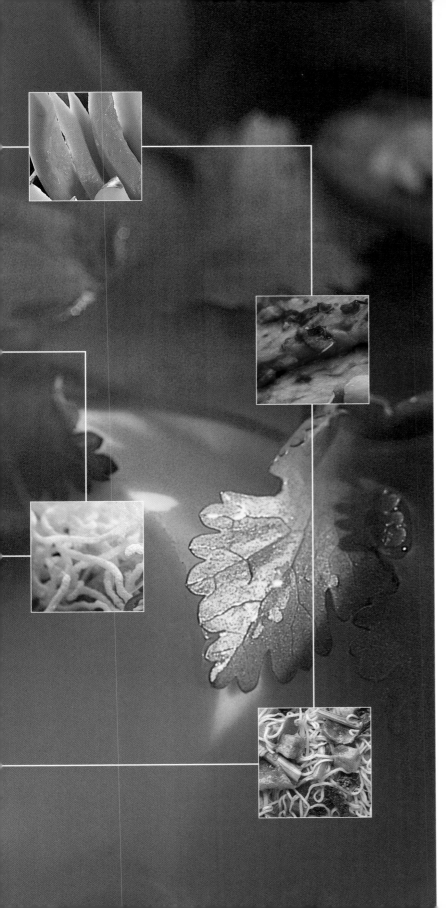

SOUTH-EAST ASIA

*I*n Thai cuisine, most soups are served as a side dish as part of a full meal. They are meant to be light and refreshing to counter-balance heavier, richer dishes. My vegetarian version of the well-known tom yum is full of bold, strong flavours like coriander roots, lemon grass, chili, kaffir lime leaves and the sour, spinach-like vegetable sorrel.

Preparation & cooking time: 20 minutes

Serves: 6 persons

- 4 scraped coriander roots
- 4 sticks lemon grass, white parts only
- 1 teaspoon yellow asafetida powder
- 2 or 3 small fresh hot red chilies, chopped
- 2 litres/quarts rich vegetable stock (recipe follows)
- 4 kaffir lime leaves
- 4 large ripe tomatoes, blanched, peeled and coarsely chopped
- 400g (13 ounces) firm pressed tofu, cut into 2.5cm (1-inch) pieces
- 1 bunch sorrel, torn
- 2 or 3 small fresh hot red chilies, extra, sliced diagonally
- 5 tablespoons soy sauce
- ½ cup lime juice
- ⅔ cup chopped fresh coriander leaves

Hot & Sour Tom Yum Soup

Pound the coriander roots, lemon grass, asafetida and chili to a rough paste using a mortar and pestle. Alternatively, process in a blender with a few drops of water.

Boil the vegetable stock in a saucepan over full heat. Drop in the kaffir lime leaves and tomato and cook for 2 or 3 minutes.

Add the spice paste, reduce the heat to a simmer, add the tofu and sorrel and cook for another 2 minutes.

Serve: Divide the extra chili, the soy sauce, lime juice and chopped coriander into large deep serving bowls and pour the boiling soup over. Serve with hot steamed rice.

Vegetable Stock

This is a basic Vietnamese vegetable stock known as nuoc leo rau cai. I use it as a basis for many of my Asian soups.

- 4 litres/quarts water
- 1 cup carrots, sliced
- 1 cup cabbage, sliced
- ½ cup celery stalk, sliced
- ¼ cup white radish, sliced
- 1½ teaspoons salt

Combine all the ingredients in a saucepan and boil for 1 hour, or until the liquid has reduced by half.

Strain and set aside.

*L*aksa is a taste sensation — a delicious one-pot soupy combination of mild, chili-hot, rich, aromatic and delicate flavours, and a tantalising combination of crunchy, soft and milky textures. There are many versions of laksa served throughout the Malaysian peninsula. This is my hearty vegetarian version.

An essential ingredient for the authentic laksa taste is a fresh herb known as daun laksa or daun kesom — literally laksa leaf. It is available from Malaysian food suppliers. It is also available from Vietnamese providores where it is known as rau ram, or Vietnamese mint. Although it is not a true mint, it is sold as a popular Vietnamese salad herb.

Curried Malay Noodles

Laksa

Preparation & cooking time:
50-60 minutes

Serves: 6-8 persons

The curry

- ¾ cup liquid tamarind puree
- 1 cup stringless beans or snake beans cut into short lengths
- 400g (14 ounces) fried tofu, cubed
- 1 tablespoon cumin seeds
- 1 tablespoon coriander seeds
- 5 or 6 large dried red chilies
- 3 tablespoons oil
- one 5cm (2-inch) cube fresh peeled ginger, shredded
- one 2.5cm (1-inch) cube fresh peeled galangal, shredded
- finely sliced white inner stems of 2 or 3 stalks of lemon grass
- 1½ teaspoons yellow asafetida powder
- 5-6 medium tomatoes, peeled and chopped
- 1 tablespoon Malay curry powder
- 1 teaspoon freshly-ground black pepper

- 2 cups potatoes cut into cubes
- 1½ cups carrots, bias cut into thin rings
- 2 cups rich vegetable stock
- 2-3 tablespoons palm sugar
- 2 teaspoons salt
- 4 cups thick coconut milk

The noodles

- 1kg (2.2 pounds) fresh rice noodles, or 350g (12 ounces) dried rice vermicelli

The garnish

- 2 cups bean sprouts
- 2 small seedless green cucumbers, unpeeled, cut into matchstick strips
- 1 small bunch laksa leaves, finely shredded
- coarsely-ground black pepper
- lime wedges
- sambal oelek, hot chili paste (optional)

Prepare the curry:

Place the beans and a little water in a small saucepan and steam the beans for 10 minutes or until tender. Drain and set the beans aside.

Dry-roast the cumin seeds, coriander seeds and dried chilies in a small saucepan or non-stick frying pan over moderately low heat for 5 minutes or until fragrant and slightly dark. Place the spices in a spice mill or coffee grinder and grind them to a powder. Set the powder aside.

Heat the oil in a 5-litre/quart heavy-based saucepan over moderate heat. When hot, add the shredded ginger and galangal. Fry for 2-3 minutes or until opaque and fragrant. Add the sliced lemon grass, fry for another minute, or until fragrant. Sprinkle in the yellow asafetida powder, fry momentarily, then add the tomatoes. Stirring occasionally, cook the tomatoes for 5-10 minutes, or until they are soft and broken down, and the oil is visible.

Add the dry-roasted spices, the curry powder, black pepper, potato, carrot and vegetable stock. Stir to combine. Cover with the lid, bring to the boil, reduce the heat, and simmer for 5-10 minutes, or until the vegetables are tender.

Cook the noodles briefly in lightly salted boiling water, or according to directions while the curry is cooking. Drain and keep hot.

Add the tamarind purée to the simmering curry, then add the cooked beans, the sugar, salt, fried tofu, and the coconut milk. Allow the mixture to almost come to the boil, stir through gently, and remove the saucepan from the heat.

Assemble the laksa curry:

Scoop a large handful of hot noodles into each individual pre-warmed serving bowl.

Ladle on the curry.

Garnish with bean sprouts, cucumber, shredded laksa leaves and black pepper. Serve with wedges of lime and optional sambal oelek.

Balado Terong is a spicy eggplant dish from Padang, the capital of West Sumatra Province in Western Java. The enterprising Minangkabau people of West Sumatra have taken their rich, spicy cuisine called Masakan Padang and made it famous by setting up restaurants all over Indonesia and, indeed, all over the world. This cuisine is characterised by plenty of rich coconut milk and chilies. Serve Balado Terong with plain rice.

Spicy Javanese Eggplant

Balado Terong

Preparation & cooking time:
about 30 minutes

Serves: 4 persons

- 6 small thin eggplants cut into thick rings
- oil for deep frying
- 3 large tomatoes, cut in quarters
- 3 or 4 large red chilies
- 2 tablespoons oil
- two small chunks galangal root,
- half a blade fresh lemon grass
- small handful curry leaves
- 2 tablespoons palm sugar
- 1 teaspoon salt

Blend the tomatoes and whole chilies together in a blender or food processor until smooth. Remove the purée and set it aside.

Heat the oil for deep-frying in a wok or pan over high heat until fairly hot.

Fry the eggplant pieces in 2 or 3 batches, until they are tender enough to pierce with a point of a knife. Set the eggplants aside to drain.

Heat another 2 tablespoons oil in a pan or wok over moderate heat. When hot, drop in the galangal and lemon grass. Fry for one minute, or until fragrant. Add the curry leaves, fry momentarily, then add the tomato and chili mixture.

Cook for 5 or 10 minutes, or until thick and saucy. Add the sugar and salt, stir to dissolve, and gently fold in the eggplant pieces.

Serve balado terong hot with rice.

*T*his version of the exotic Gado Gado salad, popular throughout Indonesia, can be served as a side salad to accompany a main meal for four persons, or as a main dish for two persons. Obtain the Chinese bok choy, coconut milk and the tofu from any well-stocked Chinese or Asian grocer. This salad is served with a steaming-hot peanut dressing.

Preparation & cooking time: 40 minutes

Serves: 2-4 persons

- 250g (9 ounces) Chinese bok choy leaves washed and cut into bite-sized pieces
- 125g (4½ ounces) mung bean shoots
- 2 or 3 small new potatoes
- 1 cup stringless green beans cut into 3.75 cm (1½-inch) lengths
- oil for deep-frying
- 450g (1 pound) firm tofu, cut into small cubes
- ¾ cup raw peanuts
- 4 Brazil nuts
- 1 teaspoon chili powder, (more for a hotter sauce)
- ½ teaspoon yellow asafetida powder
- 1 teaspoon salt
- 1 teaspoon brown sugar
- ½ cup coconut milk
- ½ medium cucumber, unpeeled and cut into thick batons
- 1 small bunch watercress, washed and separated
- 1 tablespoon fresh lime or lemon juice
- 1 cup cold water

Indonesian Gado Gado Salad

Blanch the bok choy leaves in boiling water for about 1 minute. Rinse in cold water and drain well.

Blanch the bean shoots in a similar fashion, but for just 30 seconds. Rinse and drain.

Cook the potatoes whole in lightly salted boiling water until soft; then peel them and cut them into bite-sized pieces.

Cook the beans in lightly salted boiling water for five minutes; then drain and allow to cool.

Heat the oil in a small pan or wok over moderate heat. When fairly hot, 185°C/365°F, deep-fry the cubes of tofu until slightly golden. Remove them with a slotted spoon and drain in a colander.

Reduce the oil temperature to about 180°C/355°F and deep-fry the peanuts until golden (2 to 3 minutes). Remove and drain.

Deep-fry the Brazil nuts until golden (about 3 minutes) and drain.

Combine the chili powder, asafetida, fried nuts, salt, and sugar in a food processor and blend to a smooth powder. Add 1 cup cold water to the blended ingredients.

Transfer the contents of the blender to a heavy pan, bring to the boil, and simmer for 5 minutes. Add the coconut milk and lime juice and remove from the heat.

Serve: pile the Chinese bok choy leaves, bean shoots, potatoes, beans, tofu, cucumber, and watercress in individual neat piles on a large plate. Pour the hot peanut sauce over the salad. Serve immediately. The dressing may be served separately.

Preparation & cooking time: about 15 minutes

Serves: 4 persons

- ½ cup snake beans, sliced into small sections
- ½ cup roasted peanuts
- 3 or 4 hot green chilies
- 1 tablespoon palm sugar
- 2 tablespoons fresh lime or lemon juice
- 1 medium-sized tomato, quartered
- 200g (7 ounces) green papaya, peeled and shredded into long fine shreds
- 1 teaspoon yellow asafetida powder
- 1 teaspoon sea salt
- 2 tablespoons chopped fresh coriander leaves

*G*reen papaya is a popular ingredient in Thai cooking. This is my less aggressive version of a bold flavoured dish from North-east Thailand that's usually served with a main course and plain rice. The dressing is traditionally pounded coarsely on a large stone mortar yielding a salad with a hot, sour, salty flavour with a hint of sweetness. Green papaya can be obtained at any Asian specialty store when in season.

Thai-style Green Papaya Salad

Steam the beans over boiling water until tender. Set them aside to cool.

Prepare the dressing: place the roasted peanuts, chili, palm sugar, lime juice and tomato in a food processor fitted with a metal blade. Coarsely chop the contents with a few quick on/off bursts, then scrape the dressing into a small bowl.

Combine the cooled steamed beans, the papaya and the dressing in a bowl. Add the yellow asafetida powder, the salt and half the chopped coriander. Mix well.

Serve immediately, garnished with the remaining coriander leaves.

The beauty of this delicious salad is its simplicity

Salad of Vietnamese Greens

Preparation & cooking time: 15 minutes

Serves: 4 persons

- 200g (7 ounces) bean sprouts
- 1 packed cup basil leaves
- ¾ packed cup Vietnamese mint leaves
- ¾ packed cup coriander leaves
- 2 fresh small red chilies, sliced
- 1 lime, quartered

Wash and thoroughly drain all the vegetables and herbs.

Combine all the ingredients.

Serve on 4 individual platters with a wedge of lime.

NOTE: Vietnamese mint is also known as *rau ram* (pronounced row-ram) and laksa leaf.

*I*n Thailand, the home of this dish, the ingredients vary according to what's in season and what's on hand, and is very much open to improvisation. Knowing this, I made up a vegetarian version. Mee krob is always a big favourite at parties and special event dinners because of the way it looks — colourful, sweet and sour vegetables mounted on noodles that puff up dramatically when deep fried.

Preparation & cooking time: 35 minutes

Serves: 4 persons

- peanut oil for deep frying
- 125g (4 ounces) rice vermicelli
- 1 tablespoon minced fresh ginger
- 1 hot red chili, minced
- ½ teaspoon yellow asafetida powder
- 1 large carrot cut into long matchsticks
- 120g (4 ounces) snake beans, cut into 2cm (1-inch) lengths
- 1 large zucchini cut into 2cm (1-inch) batons
- 2 small capsicums (peppers) cut into 1cm (½-inch) cubes
- 150g (5 ounces) fried bean curd puffs, cut into 1cm (½-inch) cubes
- 100g (3 ounces) bean sprouts

Crispy Fried Noodles with Sweet & Sour Sauce

Mee Krob

Sauce

- 2 tablespoons palm sugar, grated fine
- ½ teaspoon freshly-cracked black pepper
- ¼ cup fresh lime juice
- 1 teaspoon sambal oelek
- 1 tablespoon sweet chili sauce
- 4 tablespoons vegetarian oyster sauce

Garnish

- 2 fresh red chilies, sliced
- ½ cup coriander leaves
- a few bean shoots

Whisk together all the sauce ingredients in a small bowl until the sugar dissolves. Set aside.

Heat oil in a wok over full heat until almost smoking. Cut the rice vermicelli into manageable lengths with scissors.

Deep-fry a handful of noodles at a time. The noodles will immediately puff up — remove them immediately, and place in a colander. Pour off most of the oil, leaving 1 tablespoon. Return the wok to the heat.

Fry the ginger and chilies for 1-2 minutes, or until aromatic. Sprinkle in the yellow asafetida

powder followed by the carrots and a couple of table-spoons of water. Cover the wok and steam the carrots for 2 minutes. Drop in the beans and zucchini, and replace the lid. Cook for another 2 minutes. Lift the lid, throw in the capsicums and tofu. Fry uncovered, stirring occasionally, for 1 minute. Add the sprouts.

Stir in the sauce. Cook for 30 seconds more then remove from the heat.

Serve: Place most of the fried noodles on a large serving platter. Pour on the vegetable sauce, and scatter with the reserved chili, coriander leaves and bean sprouts. Top with the rest of the crisp noodles, bring to the table and serve. Even better — fry the noodles in front of the guests.

Tempe is a cheesy substance made by soaking and boiling soya beans, inoculating them with a fungus Rhizopus oligosporus, packing them into thin slabs wrapped in polythene (or banana leaves pierced with holes) and leaving to ferment. Tempe is easily digested, delicious and a great source of protein, and best fried for optimum taste and texture.

Grilled Tempe & Mixed Leaves with Black Bean Dressing

Soak the black beans in cold water for 10 minutes. Drain, rinse and chop finely.

Whisk the chopped beans with all the other dressing ingredients.

Blanch the snow peas in boiling water for 20 seconds, drain and refresh under cold running water, then cut into long thin strips.

Slice the cucumber and carrot into long thin strips by pressing firmly with a vegetable peeler.

Combine the snow peas, cucumber, carrot, salad leaves, rocket, peanuts and coriander, and toss gently to combine.

Heat the oil in a pan or wok and deep-fry the tempe slices until golden brown, then drain.

Serve: Place salad mixture on serving plates, top with sliced warm tempe, drizzle with dressing and scatter with snow pea sprouts.

Dressing

- 2 tablespoons Chinese black beans
- ½ teaspoon yellow asafetida powder
- 2 teaspoons finely-grated fresh ginger
- 1½ tablespoons soy sauce
- ½ teaspoon sambal oelek
- ¼ cup olive oil
- 1½ tablespoons freshly-squeezed lime juice
- 2 teaspoons palm sugar, finely-grated, or brown sugar

Preparation & cooking time: 30 minutes

Serves: 4 persons

- 100g (4 ounces) snow peas
- 1 Lebanese cucumber
- 1 carrot, peeled
- 50g (2 ounces) mesclun (mixed salad leaves), about 1 packed cup
- 50g (2 ounces) rocket leaves, about 1 packed cup
- 50g (2 ounces) chopped roasted peanuts, about ⅓ cup
- ⅓ cup coriander leaves
- oil for deep-frying
- 750g (1½ pounds) tempe, cut into long thin slices
- 50g (2 ounces) snow pea sprouts, about ⅔ cup

Although rice is the staple diet of most of the people of Indonesia, corn is another important mainstay, especially in the drier eastern provinces, and also during the dry season in the whole of Indonesia. Corn is prepared in many ways, this being one of the most tasty. Serve crispy perkedel jagung alongside rice dishes, accompanied with a chutney or pickle, or alone with just a squeeze of lemon.

Preparation & cooking time:
40-50 minutes

Makes: about
25 fritters

- 2½ cups raw corn kernels fresh from the cob, about 3 or 4 large cobs
- 3 large hot green chilies, seeded and chopped
- ½ cup plain flour
- ½ cup rice flour
- ¼ teaspoon baking powder
- 2 teaspoons salt
- 2 teaspoons coriander powder
- 1 teaspoon sugar
- ½ teaspoon cayenne pepper or chili powder
- 1 teaspoon yellow asafetida powder
- oil for frying
- 6 candle nuts or large macadamia nuts
- up to ¾ cup cold water
- packed ½ cup chopped celery leaves and stalk

Indonesian Crispy Corn Fritters

Perkedel Jagung

Coarsely chop or crush the corn kernels to form a mixture of whole and semi-crushed pieces.

Combine the flour, rice flour, baking powder, salt, coriander powder, sugar, cayenne and yellow asafetida powder in a large bowl.

Heat a few tablespoons of oil in a small saucepan over moderate heat. Drop in the candlenuts or macadamia nuts and fry them until they are golden brown and aromatic. Remove, drain and slightly cool the nuts.

Grind the nuts to a powder in a spice mill or coffee grinder.

Add three-quarters of the water to the bowl of flour and spices, and whisk it to form a very thick batter. Fold in the corn, the nut powder, the celery, and the chilies. Adjust the consistency with extra water, if required, to form a thick but spoonable batter.

Heat oil in a 22.5cm (9-inch) frying pan to a depth of 1.25cm (½-inch) over moderate heat. When the oil is fairly hot, carefully spoon in 6-8 heaped tablespoons of batter, flattening them into circular fritters.

Shallow fry the fritters for 3 or 4 minutes or until the undersides of the fritters are golden brown. Turn the fritters over with kitchen tongs and fry them until the other side is also golden brown. Remove and place on absorbent paper towels to dry.

Repeat for all the fritters, and serve hot.

Our recipe-testing crew polished off these Malaysian delicacies in record time. If you're looking for a finger food par excellence, seek no further.

Preparation & cooking time: 40-50 minutes

Makes: about 40 bite-size puffs

- 1 cup sweet potato, diced very small
- 1 cup carrot, diced very small
- 1 cup potato, diced very small
- 1 cup peas
- 2 tablespoons ghee or oil
- fresh curry leaves from 3 large sprigs, torn
- 1 tablespoon grated fresh ginger
- ½ teaspoon yellow asafetida powder
- 2 tablespoons Malaysian hot curry powder
- 2 teaspoons sugar
- 1 teaspoon salt
- 5 sheets ready-made puff pastry
- ghee or oil for deep frying
- quick tamarind chutney, to serve (recipe follows)

Curry Puffs with Quick Tamarind Chutney

The filling:

Steam the vegetables separately until tender. Drain.

Heat the ghee or oil in a frying pan over moderate heat. When the oil is hot, drop in the curry leaves and fry until they crackle, sprinkle in the ginger, fry for 1 minute or until aromatic, then add the yellow asafetida powder and fry momentarily.

Stir in the curry powder, all the cooked vegetables, the sugar and the salt. Fry together for 1 or 2 minutes then remove from the heat. Allow the mixture to cool.

The puffs:

Cut the sheets of puff pastry into 8cm (3-inch) rounds with a pastry cutter.

Place 2 teaspoons of cooled filling in the centre of each square. Fold into semi-circles and seal, leaving the edge plain, pressed with fork tines, or with a decorative pinched and fluted edge.

Heat the ghee or oil for deep-frying in a wok or deep frying pan over moderate heat until fairly hot.

Fry the puffs in batches for 2-3 minutes or until puffed and golden brown. Remove and drain on paper towels.

Serve hot, warm or cold with the accompanying tamarind chutney or sweet chili sauce.

Quick Tamarind Chutney

Simultaneously hot, sweet, sour and spicy.

Makes: 1 cup chutney

- ¼ cup dried tamarind, soaked in 2 cups boiling water for ½ hour
- ½ teaspoon ground cumin
- 2 teaspoons ginger juice (juice squeezed from about 2 tablespoons shredded ginger)
- 3 tablespoons brown sugar
- ½ teaspoon salt
- big pinch chili powder

Pour the soaked tamarind through a sieve, collecting all the juice. Rub and squeeze the remaining pulp to extract all the tamarind purée. Discard the dry residue.

Combine the tamarind purée with all the remaining ingredients in a medium saucepan. Cook over moderately high heat for 10-15 minutes, or until reduced by half. Serve at room temperature.

The basis of this chili-hot noodle dish is dried Chinese-style wheat noodles known as mie. They can be obtained in any Asian grocery or most good supermarkets. The chili-hot taste of this well known Malaysian Chinese dish comes from sambal oelek, a condiment made from minced fresh red chilies and salt. The dried tofu that I use comes in the form of thick rectangular sheets about 5 cm x 10 cm (2 inches x 4 inches) and is called teem chook. Select young, thin-stalked choy sum, cut off 2.5 cm (1-inch) from the base and use the rest.

Malaysian Hot Noodles with Tofu
Mie Goreng

Preparation & cooking time:
20-30 minutes

Serves: 8 persons

- 375g (13 ounces) thick dried tofu rectangles teem chook
- 250g (9 ounces) Chinese dried wheat noodles
- oil for deep frying
- 400g (14 ounces) firm tofu cut into 1.25 cm (½-inch) cubes
- 3 tablespoons peanut oil
- 3 tablespoons minced fresh ginger
- ½ teaspoon yellow asafetida powder
- 1 bunch choy sum, chopped into 2.5 cm (1-inch) sections (leaves and stalks)
- 3 tablespoons soy sauce
- 2 tablespoons plain sambal oelek (or more if you want hotter noodles)
- 3 tablespoons fresh lemon juice
- 2 cups mung bean shoots
- 1 tablespoon Chinese sesame oil

Soak the dried tofu rectangles in hot water for 15 minutes. When softened, cut into 2.5 cm (1-inch) squares, drain, and pat dry.

Cook the wheat noodles according to the directions on the packet until they are still a little firm (al dente). Drain, rinse under cold water, and drain again.

Heat the oil in a wok or pan over high heat. Deep-fry the tofu cubes until they turn golden brown, remove, and drain. Repeat for all the tofu.

Deep-fry the dried tofu until golden and slightly blistered. Remove and drain.

Heat the peanut oil in another wok over full heat. Sauté the minced ginger for 1 minute. Add the asafetida and choy sum and stir-fry until the vegetables become soft.

Add the soy sauce, sambal oelek, lemon juice, fried dry tofu, fried fresh tofu, bean shoots and sesame oil and stir well. Increase the heat and add the drained wheat noodles. Stir-fry for another 2 minutes or until the noodles are hot.

Serve the noodles hot.

*A*lso known as kuih buah melaka, these delicious dumplings derive their pleasantly chewy texture from glutinous rice flour. All the ingredients for onde-onde are available at Asian supermarkets.

Preparation & cooking time: 35-40 minutes

Makes: 20 dumplings

- one 20cm (8-inch) strip of fresh or frozen pandan leaf
- few drops green colouring
- 1¼ cups glutinous (sticky) rice flour
- ¼ cup plus 1½ tablespoons boiling water
- 60g (2 ounces) palm sugar cut into small pieces
- 1 cup freshly-grated coconut mixed with a pinch salt

Indonesian Sticky Coconut Dumplings

Onde-Onde

Pound and squeeze the pandan leaf in a mortar and pestle with 2 tablespoons of hot water to extract its fragrant juice.

Sift the glutinous rice flour into a bowl.

Pour in a combination of the boiling water and 1 tablespoon of the pandan juice mixed with the green food colouring. Mix well and knead into a firm lump of dough.

Roll the mixture into marble-size balls. Flatten each ball slightly and insert 1 or 2 pieces of palm sugar. Fully enclose the sugar, and re-shape into

balls, making sure that the dough is fully sealed with no cracks or exposed sugar. If cracks appear, simply moisten them with water and seal again.

Bring water to the boil in a large saucepan, and drop in half the balls. When cooked, the balls will rise to the surface. Remove them with a slotted spoon, shake them dry and immediately roll them in the grated coconut.

Serve warm or cold.

The pandan leaf (sometimes referred to as screw pine) is an aromatic member of the pandanus family. After tying each leaf in a knot, they are often added to Indonesian, Malay and Nyonya rice and sweet dishes, while the juice is extracted for sweetmeats known in Malaysia as kuis, of which the above are a famous example.

This simple and sublime dessert is popular, in one form or another, all over South-East Asia. In Thailand, where it is known as khaoneow mamuang, it is eaten not just as a dessert, but as a sweet afternoon snack, or any time.

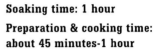

Thai Sticky Rice with Mango

Soaking time: 1 hour

Preparation & cooking time: about 45 minutes-1 hour

Serves: 4 persons

- 2 cups sticky (glutinous) white rice, soaked in cold water for 1 hour, then drained
- 1¼ cups coconut milk
- pinch salt
- 2 tablespoons sugar
- 2 large ripe mangoes
- 2 tablespoons coconut milk to serve
- mint leaves to decorate

Combine the rice, coconut milk, salt and sugar in an uncovered saucepan with 1¼ cups of water. Stir and bring to the boil over moderate heat.

Simmer the rice, stirring, for about 8-10 minutes, or until all the liquid has been absorbed. Remove from the heat, cover the pan, and leave it to stand for 5 minutes.

Transfer the rice to a steamer or double saucepan, and steam it for 15-20 minutes.

Spoon the hot steamed sticky rice into 6-8 individual ramekins or individual pudding moulds lined with plastic wrap and set them aside to cool.

Serve: Remove the rice from the mould, and place one portion in the centre of each dessert plate. Arrange the mango around it, and drizzle the rice with the reserved coconut milk. Garnish with mint leaves.

NOTE: as an alternative serving suggestion, press the warm rice evenly into a tray lined with plastic wrap. When cold cut into diamond-shaped pieces.

Sticky rice can be served with a variety of fruits — typically mango, jackfruit or durian. It is also sometimes eaten with palm sugar syrup, with thick coconut milk and a pinch of salt, sprinkled with sesame, or served with a type of coconut milk custard called sankhaya. You can even serve it with sweetened or unsweetened cream.

**Preparation time:
about 30 minutes**

Serves: 6-8 persons

The dipping sauce

- ¼ cup liquid tamarind purée
- ½ cup roasted peanuts
- 3 hot green chilies, seeded
- 1 tablespoon fresh lime or lemon juice
- 250g (9 ounces) palm sugar, or brown sugar
- 1½ teaspoons salt

The fruit selection

- 500g (a little over a pound) each of 5 or 6 of the following fruits, cut into large bite-size chunks: pineapple, red or yellow papaya, bangkwang or apple, rose apple, or pear, banana, honeydew melon, cantaloupe, or any other firm fruit

*T*his is a very popular dish amongst Indonesian women and girls, and especially expectant mothers. Rujak means any kind of mixed fruit or vegetable salad with a spicy sauce, sometimes containing ground peanuts, and manis means sweet. Rujak manis is often sold door-to-door by street vendors, and is also readily available in the busy city streets. The fruits are freshly cut and the sauce spooned on top, keeping the fresh individual tastes of the fruits intact. When I first tasted this dish, the fruit selection contained rose apple and bangkwang, also known as yam bean, or jicama. These fruits are sometimes hard to come by in non-tropical countries, so I have suggested some alternatives.

Fruit Platter with Hot & Sweet Dipping Sauce

Rujak Manis

Grind the peanuts in a food processor until smooth. Add the chilies, tamarind purée, lime juice, palm sugar and salt. Process to a smooth, sauce-like consistency. You may need to add a few drops of water.

Set aside this sauce for 10 minutes for the flavours to mingle.

Arrange the fruits on a platter with the sauce in a separate bowl, along with skewers or toothpicks, allowing diners to dip the fruits or pour the sauce onto the fruits as they desire.

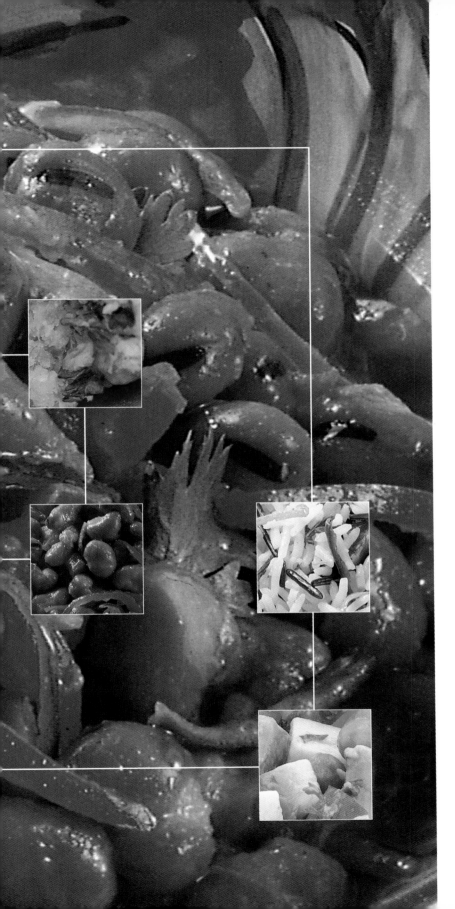

This chilled soup is very refreshing on a hot day, and requires practically no cooking.

**Preparation & cooking time:
30 minutes**

Serves: 4-6 persons

- 1 large peeled cucumber diced into 0.5cm (¼-inch) cubes (reserve one-third)

- 1 small green pepper, diced into 0.5cm (¼-inch) cubes (reserve 1 tablespoon)

- 2 large fresh ripe tomatoes, diced (reserve half)

- 2 tablespoons extra virgin olive oil (reserve 1 teaspoon)

- 1 teaspoon salt

- 1 tablespoon fresh lemon juice

- ¼ teaspoon yellow asafetida powder (reserve)

- 2 teaspoons honey

- ½ teaspoon dried dill

- ¼ teaspoon cayenne pepper

- 2 tablespoons eggless mayonnaise

- 2 cups tomato juice

- 2 tablespoons chopped fresh coriander, garnish

- 2 tablespoons chopped fresh parsley, as garnish

Mexican Chilled Vegetable Soup

Gazpacho

Combine the reserved cucumber, peppers and tomatoes and set aside.

Blend the remaining ingredients — the cucumbers, peppers, tomatoes, most of the oil, the salt, lemon juice, honey, dill, cayenne, mayonnaise, and tomato juice — in a blender or food processor until the mixture is nearly smooth. Empty the contents of the blender into a large bowl.

Heat the remaining olive oil in a medium-sized pan over moderate heat. Sauté the asafetida in the hot oil. Turn off the heat. Add the reserved cucumber, the reserved green pepper, and the reserved tomato pieces to the hot pan. Stir them once and add them to the puréed soup. Mix well. Refrigerate.

Serve garnished with the parsley and coriander in chilled soup bowls.

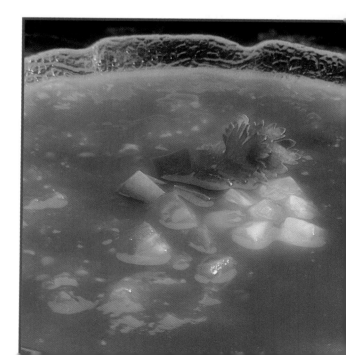

Avocados combine well with cheese and beans. Dressed and served in lettuce leaves, this salad is substantial and tasty.

Avocado & Bean Salad

Combine the avocados, beans, chickpeas, cheese, green pepper, and pimientos in a bowl.

Mix the olive oil, lemon juice, honey, half the parsley, coriander, black pepper, and salt.

Fold the dressing carefully into the bean and avocado mixture. Serve individual portions of salad on lettuce leaves and garnish with the remaining chopped parsley.

Preparation time:
10 minutes

Serves: 8 persons

- 2 large ripe avocados, peeled and cut into small cubes
- 1 cup cooked and chilled green beans chopped into short sections
- 1 cup cooked and chilled kidney beans
- 1 cup cooked and chilled chickpeas
- 1 cup cubed cheddar cheese
- ½ cup chopped green pepper (capsicum)
- ¼ cup chopped pimiento (baby red peppers in brine or oil)
- ⅔ cup olive oil
- ⅔ cup fresh lemon juice
- 3 tablespoons honey
- 2 teaspoons chopped fresh parsley
- 2 teaspoons chopped fresh coriander leaves
- ½ teaspoon black pepper
- 1 teaspoon salt
- 1 large Iceberg, Cos, or Mignonette lettuce to serve

Preparation time:
10 minutes

Refrigeration time:
at least 1 hour

Serves: 4-6 persons

- flesh from 3 medium-sized ripe avocados
- 1 teaspoon salt
- 1 tablespoon fresh lime or lemon juice
- ½ teaspoon yellow asafetida powder
- 1 tablespoon fresh coriander leaves
- 4 cups rich vegetable stock, or more for a thinner soup
- 1 tablespoon green peppercorns preserved in brine, drained and rinsed
- ½ cup crème fraîche
- extra ¼ cup crème fraîche for garnish
- extra 1 tablespoon coriander leaves for garnish
- a few green peppercorns for garnish

Green peppercorns are picked unripe, and are usually preserved in brine. They have an invigorating, lively taste and combine well with the delicate flavour of avocados. This velvety-smooth chilled soup is an ideal addition to a summer menu. It is uncooked and practically effortless to prepare. Select ripe but blemish-free avocados that feel heavy for their size.

Chilled Avocado & Green Peppercorn Soup

Process the avocados, salt, lime juice, yellow asafetida powder, coriander leaves, half the stock, 2 teaspoons of the peppercorns, and the cream to a smooth purée in a food processor. Add the remaining stock and process again. Add a little extra stock now if you desire a thinner consistency.

Pour the soup into a large bowl. Fold in the other 2 teaspoons green peppercorns. Cover and refrigerate for at least 1 hour.

Serve the soup in individual bowls with a swirl of the reserved crème fraîche, a few peppercorns and the garnish of fresh coriander leaves.

The sweet potato, like the ordinary potato, was cultivated in pre-historic Peru. It is now grown around the world and comes in hundreds of varieties, the most common being yellow and white. As a general rule, the paler the colour, the drier the flesh. The darker tubers become more moist and sweet when cooked.

Whichever variety of sweet potato you prefer, they combine beautifully with another South American favourite — fresh corn. For contrasting texture, I have left the corn kernels whole in this heart-warming soup. If you prefer, you can blend the corn to a purée with the sweet potatoes.

Sweet Potato Soup with Corn & Chilies

Preparation & cooking time: about 40 minutes

Serves: 4-6 persons

- ¼ cup butter
- 1 teaspoon yellow asafetida powder
- 4-5 cups sweet potato, diced
- 4 cups rich vegetable stock
- 1¼ cups cooked corn kernels
- 1 green jalapeño chili, seeded and finely diced
- 1½ teaspoons salt (less if using a salty stock)
- ½ teaspoon freshly-ground black pepper
- whole coriander leaves for garnish

Heat the butter in a 3-litre/quart saucepan over moderate heat. Sprinkle in the yellow asafetida powder and drop in the sweet potatoes. Fry the potatoes for 2 or 3 minutes, then add the vegetable stock. Bring to the boil and cook for 15-20 minutes, or until the sweet potatoes are tender but not broken down. Remove the saucepan from the heat. Strain the sweet potatoes, being careful to reserve all the liquid. Return the cooking liquid to the rinsed-out saucepan.

Process the sweet potatoes along with some of the cooking liquid in a food processor and reduce them to a purée.

Add the sweet potato purée to the cooking liquid and return to moderate heat. Add the cooked corn, chili, salt and pepper.

Simmer the soup for another 10 minutes.

Serve hot with crusty bread and a garnish of fresh coriander leaves.

*A*rroz verde (literally "green rice") is coloured with spinach, fresh parsley and coriander leaves, and flavoured with fresh, very mild, large green chilies, such as poblano or anaheim. If these chili varieties are unavailable, use any large, mild green chilies that you can find.

Mexican Green Chili Rice
Arroz Verde

Roast the chilies over a burning gas jet on your stove holding them with a pair of kitchen tongs, (or place under the griller) until they brown a little. Transfer them to a plastic bag. Seal the bag. When cool, carefully remove the chilies, peel them, remove the seeds and cut them into thin strips. Put aside in a small bowl.

Process the spinach leaves and half the herbs in a food processor with a little of the vegetable stock. Blend to a purée.

Transfer this green purée, along with the remaining stock and the salt to a 2-litre/quart saucepan over moderate heat and bring it to the boil.

Heat the oil in another 2-litre/quart saucepan over moderate heat. When hot, sprinkle in the yellow asafetida powder, stir momentarily, then add the rice and fry for 2 or 3 minutes, or until translucent.

Pour in the boiling vegetable stock. Increase the heat to full, bring to the boil, cover with a lid, and reduce the heat to a gentle simmer.

Cook the rice without stirring for 15-20 minutes, or until the grains are soft, dry and tender.

Remove the pan from the heat and set aside for 5 minutes. Remove the lid, stir in the remaining herbs and black pepper.

Serve hot, garnishing each serve with strips of roasted chilies.

Preparation & cooking time: about 40 minutes

Serves: 4-6 persons

- 3 large mild fresh green chilies
- 3 or 4 large spinach leaves thoroughly washed and drained
- 1 cup chopped parsley
- ½ cup chopped fresh coriander leaves
- 3 cups vegetable broth or stock
- 1½ teaspoons salt
- 2-3 tablespoons olive oil
- ½ teaspoon yellow asafetida powder
- 1½ cups long-grain white rice
- ¼ teaspoon coarsely-ground black pepper

*H*ash browns are a well-known American breakfast food. Although generally quite plain, this version is spiked with fresh thyme, lemon zest and Dijon mustard. I've discovered that 7.5cm (3-inch) "egg rings" keep hash browns from disintegrating in the frying pan. They're inexpensive metal rings available from kitchenware or hardware stores — you'll need five for this recipe.

Preparation & cooking time: about 40 minutes

Makes: 10 Hash Browns

- 5 medium-sized baking-type potatoes
- 1 teaspoon salt
- 2-3 teaspoons fresh thyme leaves, chopped
- 1-2 tablespoons Dijon mustard
- 1 teaspoon finely-grated lemon rind
- ¼ teaspoon freshly-ground black pepper
- 4 tablespoons butter
- ½ teaspoon yellow asafetida powder

Pan-fried Potato Cakes

Hash Browns

Boil the potatoes in a large saucepan of lightly salted water until just cooked. Drain and allow to cool slightly. Coarsely chop. Place the potatoes in a bowl, and add the salt, pepper, thyme, mustard and lemon zest.

Heat 1 tablespoon of the butter in a small pan over low heat. Sprinkle in the yellow asafetida powder and fry momentarily. Add this seasoned butter to the potatoes. Combine the mixture well.

Melt the remaining butter in a large, non-stick frying pan over moderate heat. Place 5 lightly oiled, 7.5cm (3-inch) egg rings on the pan, and spoon the potato mixture evenly into the rings. Fill the rings to the top, and press down firmly to form flat cakes.

Fry the rings of potato for 5-7 minutes or until a crust forms on the underside. Shake the pan occasionally to avoid sticking.

Turn over the potato cakes with a spatula, and carefully remove the rings with tongs. Fry them for another 4-5 minutes, or until crusty on the second side. Remove the hash browns and place them to drain on paper towels. Repeat the procedure for the second batch and

Serve hot.

I was dubious when I was sent this recipe for chili biscuits by a little old lady from Pasadena. But she assured me they were delicious, and after cooking my first batch I had to agree.

THE AMERICAS

Cheddar & Jalapeño Chili Biscuits

Jalapeño chilies (pronounced 'halapenyo') are the rounded, fleshy variety with a medium level of heat, 5.5 on the Scoville Scale (a sort of Richter scale for chilies). They have become one of the most popular and versatile chilies around these days, and find their way into salsas, stews, salads, dressings and even biscuits.

Preheat the oven to 220°C/425°F.

Sift together the flour, cornmeal, baking powder, baking soda and salt in a bowl. Rub in the butter and combine thoroughly until the mixture resembles coarse meal. If you prefer, combine in a food processor, then turn out into a bowl.

Stir in the cheese and the chilies, add the milk and stir the mixture until it forms a soft and sticky dough.

Drop the dough by rounded tablespoons onto a buttered baking sheet.

Bake the biscuits in the centre of the preheated oven for 15-20 minutes, or until they are pale golden.

Serve at room temperature.

Preparation & cooking time: 35-40 minutes

Makes: about 18 biscuits

- 1 cup plain flour
- ½ cup yellow cornmeal (polenta)
- 2 teaspoons baking powder
- ½ teaspoon baking soda
- ½ teaspoon salt
- 2 tablespoons cold unsalted butter, cut into bits
- 1½ cups grated extra tasty cheddar cheese
- 2 or 3 pickled 4cm (1½-inch) jalapeño chilies, minced
- 2 or 3 fresh 4cm (1½-inch) jalapeño chilies, minced
- ⅔ cup milk

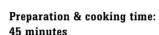

*C*hickpeas are not only packed full of valuable nutrients, they're also versatile. These attractive patties come with a tasty oven-caramelised salsa. Add a salad and you have a substantial meal. If you commence the salsa first, it should be ready to serve with the cutlets.

Preparation & cooking time:
45 minutes

Makes: 24 cutlets

- 4 cups cooked chickpeas, rinsed and drained
- ½ cup coriander leaves
- ½ cup fresh mint leaves
- 1 tablespoon chopped fresh ginger
- 3 green chilies, seeded and chopped
- 2 teaspoons ground cumin
- 2½ teaspoons salt
- 1 teaspoon freshly-cracked black pepper
- ⅔ cup fresh or frozen corn kernels
- 2 cups fresh bread crumbs
- 5 small red capsicums (peppers), roasted, peeled, seeded and diced small
- oil for pan-frying

Chickpea Cutlets with New Mexico Chili & Tomato Salsa

Combine the chickpeas, coriander, mint, ginger, chilies, cumin, salt and pepper in a food processor.

Pulse until coarsely chopped. Add the corn and pulse a little more until the corn is slightly broken. Transfer the mixture to a bowl.

Fold in the bread crumbs and diced capsicums. Mix to fully incorporate the bread crumbs. The mixture should be fairly stiff. Add more bread crumbs if necessary.

Form the mixture into 24 patties with moistened palms. Pour sufficient oil in a frying pan for pan-frying and place over moderately high heat.

Pan-fry the patties in the hot oil in batches, cooking them 3-4 minutes on each side, or until well browned. Drain on paper towels.

Serve warm with the chili and tomato salsa.

New Mexico Chili and Tomato Salsa

A full-bodied, hot and smoky salsa redolent with the earthy flavour and distinct mild heat of New Mexico chilies (sometimes referred to as Colorado or California chilies).

Makes: about 1½ cups

- 3 large dried New Mexico chilies
- 6 ripe tomatoes, blanched, peeled, seeded and chopped
- 1 tablespoon olive oil
- 1 tablespoon brown sugar

Soak the chilies in hot water for 20 minutes, or until soft. Drain them, remove the stems, and then finely chop the chilies.

Preheat the oven to 220°C/425°F.

Combine all the ingredients in an oven proof pan.

Bake for about 20 minutes or until the tomatoes start to caramelise and turn brown.

Serve at room temperature with the chickpea cutlets.

Bean soaking time: 24 hours

Preparation & cooking time: about 30 minutes

Serves: 4-6 persons

- 1¼ cups uncooked dried broad beans (fava beans) — any size or variety — soaked for 24 hours

- 4 tablespoons fresh lime juice or lemon juice

- 3 tablespoons virgin olive oil

- ½ teaspoon dried oregano

- 1½ teaspoons salt

- ¾ teaspoon yellow asafetida powder

- 3 jalapeño chilies, seeded and cut into julienne strips

- 3 tablespoons coarsely chopped fresh coriander leaves

- 1 cup finely-diced unpeeled tomatoes

- 3 tablespoons chopped fresh coriander leaves for garnish

Dried broad beans, also called fava beans, are known by the name habas in Spanish. They appear in many dishes throughout South and Central America. In this simple but hearty salad from central Mexico, fava beans are combined with chopped tomatoes, chilies and fresh coriander leaves and drenched in a tangy lime juice and olive oil dressing. For an authentic Mexican flavour, try to procure jalapeño chilies, and Mexican oregano. Fava beans are easily available from Mexican suppliers, or from Middle Eastern grocers, where they go by the name ful beans.

Mexican Broad Bean Salad

Ensalada de Habas

Drain the beans, rinse them, and drain them again.

Remove the skins from the beans if you wish. The best way is to squeeze the bean hard, a little off-centre — it should pop out of its thick skin. If it resists, tear a little skin first. If you prefer a more authentic chewy texture, miss out this step.

Bring to the boil the beans in a 3-litre/ quart saucepan with plenty of cold water over high heat. Reduce the heat and simmer the beans for about 15-20 minutes, or until they are soft. Drain the beans thoroughly, transfer to a serving bowl, and allow them to cool slightly.

Combine the lime juice, olive oil, oregano, salt and yellow asafetida powder in a small bowl.

Mix the chili strips, the chopped coriander leaves and the tomatoes with the beans.

Pour the dressing on the beans, mix well, and allow the salad to marinate for at least 45 minutes. Garnish with the extra chopped coriander and serve at room temperature.

*T*he Creoles and Cajuns of southern Louisiana have their own distinctive and spicy cuisine. This tasty cornbread, spiked with herbs and spices, is tasty and easy to prepare. Serve the bread as an accompaniment to a moist vegetable dish, or with a salad and soup for a light meal.

Spicy Cajun Cornbread

Preparation & cooking time: about 30 minutes

Makes: 1 small loaf

- 1 cup polenta
- ½ cup plain flour
- 1 tablespoon baking powder
- 1 teaspoon salt
- 1 teaspoon Spanish-style hot smoked paprika powder (or ½ teaspoon cayenne plus ½ teaspoon sweet paprika)
- ½ teaspoon yellow asafetida powder
- ¼ teaspoon dried oregano
- ¼ teaspoon dried thyme leaves
- ¼ teaspoon freshly-ground black pepper
- ¼ teaspoon white pepper
- 2 tablespoons minced fresh green chilies
- 1 cup buttermilk
- 3 tablespoons oil
- ¾ cup shredded tasty cheese

Pre-heat the oven to 220°C/430°F.

Combine the polenta, flour, baking powder, salt, paprika, yellow asafetida powder, oregano, thyme, the two peppers and chilies in a large bowl. Stir to mix well.

Whisk together the buttermilk and oil in another small bowl,

Combine the dry and moist ingredients to form a thick batter. Add the cheese and mix well.

Spoon the mixture into an oiled 17.5cm (7-inch) long loaf pan, or a 22.5cm (9-inch) pie dish. Place in the pre-heated oven.

Bake for 20 minutes, or until golden on top. Slice and serve warm.

*I*n this monumental dessert, sweet red apples are wrapped in a rich pastry and then baked in an even richer sauce. This recipe, originally from the Amish people of Pennsylvania, is definitely not diet food. The Amish are famous for their hard work. If you've been building barns or ploughing the fields all day, you won't feel guilty returning home to these deliciously saucy, individually packaged apple pies.

Amish Apple Dumplings

Combine the flour and salt into a bowl. Cut the butter into small pieces and rub it into the flour until the mixture resembles coarse meal.

Mix together the buttermilk, water and vinegar or lemon juice, and stir it into the flour mixture to form a soft pastry. Knead the dough briefly, then set it aside for a few minutes.

Roll out the pastry on a large floured surface until it's big enough to cut into 8 squares, each big enough to completely fit around an apple.

Cut the pastry into 8 squares, place an apple on one square and wrap it, lightly sealing the pastry on top. Repeat for all the apples. Place the apples on a lightly buttered 22.5cm x 32.5cm (9 inch x 13 inch) baking pan. Pre-heat the oven to 180˚C/355˚F.

Combine the butter, sugar and water in a small saucepan and bring this sauce to the boil over moderate heat.

Pour the sauce over the apple dumplings, and place the pan in the oven.

Bake for 40-50 minutes, or until the dumplings are golden brown and the apples yield easily to a knife.

Serve: the Amish like to pour cold milk over their warm dumplings. Try cream or ice cream. Happy ploughing!

Preparation & cooking time:
55 minutes-
1 hour 10 minutes
Makes: 8 apple dumplings

The apples
- 3 cups plain flour
- 1 teaspoon salt
- 1¼ cups cold butter
- 2 tablespoons buttermilk
- 2 tablespoons cold water
- 1 tablespoon vinegar or lemon juice
- 8 sweet red apples, peeled and left whole

The sauce
- ½ cup butter
- 1 cup brown sugar
- 4 tablespoons water

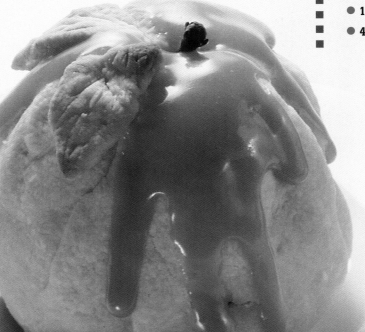

ild rice is the seed of an aquatic grass that grows in ponds, lakes and waterways of the United States and Canada. It is not actually a grain, but it is treated as such. Its long, thin, ash-brown to blackish grains cook to a chewy texture, with a slightly smoky flavour. Wild rice teams up very well with basmati rice, and in this recipe is joined by continental parsley, slivered toasted pecans, currants and orange zest. Serve as a side dish.

Preparation & cooking time: about 40 minutes

Serves: 6 persons

- ½ cup wild rice
- 1 cup basmati rice
- 1 tablespoon extra virgin olive oil
- ⅓ cup dried currants
- 1 teaspoon salt
- 2 tablespoons fresh orange juice
- ¼ teaspoon black pepper
- 2 teaspoons grated orange zest
- 3 tablespoons chopped, fresh continental parsley
- ⅓ cup pecan nuts, slivered lengthwise into thirds and pan-toasted
- 2 small green chilies, seeded and finely slivered
- sprigs of continental parsley

Pecan & Orange Wild Rice Pilaf

Bring to the boil 2 cups of water in a small saucepan over full heat. Stir in the wild rice, reduce the heat, cover the pan and simmer for about 40 minutes, or until the grains are tender. Do not allow the grains to split. Transfer the rice to a sieve and drain off the liquid. Set the rice aside.

Heat the olive oil in a 2-litre/quart saucepan over moderate heat. Add the basmati rice and currants, and gently stir-fry for 2-3 minutes, being careful not to break up the rice grains. Add 1¾ cups water to the saucepan and bring it to the boil. Add the salt, orange juice, black pepper and orange zest. Reduce the heat to a simmer.

Cook the rice, covered, for about 18 minutes or until the rice is soft and dry. Remove from the heat and set aside for 10 minutes.

Fluff the rice gently with a fork. Add the wild rice, the chopped parsley, the pecan nuts and chilies, and gently mix.

Serve immediately, garnished with the sprigs of continental parsley.

ancy something a little different for breakfast? Try these.

Corn Cakes with Maple Syrup

Combine the flour, polenta and baking powder in a large mixing bowl. Whisk in the milk, sour cream, corn kernels, salt and pepper. Allow the polenta to soak for 1 minute.

Heat a non-stick frying pan over moderate heat, drizzle in some of the melted butter, and fry ¼ cupfuls of the mixture on both sides for 3 or 4 minutes each side, or until golden brown.

Serve hot with the maple syrup.

- Preparation & cooking time: 35 minutes
- Makes: 10-12 pancakes

- ½ cup self-raising flour
- 1 cup fine polenta, or ½ cup polenta plus ½ cup fine semolina
- ½ teaspoon baking powder
- 1 cup milk
- 2 tablespoons sour cream
- corn kernels from one large cooked corn cob, about 1 cup
- 1 teaspoon salt
- ½ teaspoon freshly-ground black pepper
- 4 or 5 tablespoons melted butter
- 1 cup maple syrup for serving

This is a spicy, all-American favourite dessert. Select highly flavoured dark-fleshed pumpkins for optimum flavour. Butternut, or especially a Japanese variety — Kabocha (or Jap as it is known in Australia), is highly recommended.

Pumpkin Pie

Preparation & cooking time: about 2 hours

Makes: one 22.5cm (9-inch) pie

The crust

- 1 cup unbleached plain flour
- ⅓ cup butter
- ½ teaspoon salt
- 5-7 tablespoons cold water

The filling

- 1 medium-sized pumpkin
- one 400g (14-ounce) can sweetened condensed milk, about 1¼ cups
- 2 tablespoons cornflour (cornstarch)
- 1 teaspoon cinnamon powder
- ½ teaspoon salt
- 2 teaspoons freshly ground whole allspice berries
- ½ teaspoon freshly grated nutmeg

Prepare the pastry:

Process the flour, butter and salt in a food processor with 12-15 short bursts until it resembles coarse breadcrumbs. Sprinkle in 2 tablespoons cold water, and process with another 6 short bursts. Add another 1 or 2 tablespoons water, if required, to form a damp mass.

Remove and gather the pastry into a ball, and place it on a floured surface.

Roll out the pastry to line a 22.5cm (9-inch) pie dish or tart pan with removable bottom. Trim and crimp the edges and chill while you prepare the filling.

Prepare the filling:

Split the pumpkin crosswise. Remove and discard the seeds and fibres. Place the pumpkin, cut side down on a lightly buttered baking sheet. Place in a 160°C/320°F oven.

Bake for about 1 hour, or until the pumpkin is tender when pierced with a knife.

Scrape away the pulp from the skin, discard the skin, and place the pulp in a food processor fitted with a metal blade.

Process the pumpkin in batches until smooth.

Press the pumpkin purée through a sieve, measure 2 cups for the pie and reserve the remainder for other purposes.

Combine the measured pumpkin purée with all the other filling ingredients. Beat with a wire whisk until smooth and creamy.

Assemble and bake the pie:

Pre-heat the oven to 200°C/390°F.

Pour the filling into the chilled pastry case and smooth it out. It should be barely 2.5cm (1-inch) deep.

Bake for 40 minutes or until the filling is set.

Serve: cool, cut into wedges and serve with whipped cream.

_R_ipe papayas, whether red, orange or yellow fleshed are beautifully sweet. When choosing papayas, select fruits that are soft enough to hold an impression from gentle thumb or finger pressure. Their aroma should be pronounced and musky sweet. This refreshing drink from Guatemala is flavoured with lime and pure vanilla. If limes are unavailable, replace with lemons. Serve it icy cold. Refresco!

Chilled Papaya Refresher

Refresco de Papaya

Preparation time:
a few minutes

Serves: 4-6 persons

- 1 large ripe papaya, about 700g (1½ pounds)
- ⅔ cup very cold buttermilk or milk
- ½ cup sugar
- black pulp scraped from 1 plump vanilla bean, or 1 teaspoon vanilla sugar
- 2 cups crushed ice
- 5 tablespoons strained fresh lime juice
- ½ teaspoon finely-grated lime zest
- thin slices of lime for garnish (optional)

Peel the papaya, cut in half, remove the seeds and chop coarsely.

Process the fruit in a blender with the buttermilk or milk, sugar, vanilla and ice on high speed until the fruit is smooth. Add the lime juice, lime zest and process again until smooth and thick.

Serve: pour into tall, chilled glasses and serve at once, garnished with lime slices.

THE WORLD

This light and delicious tomato soup makes the canned variety pale into insignificance. Prepared from fresh ripe tomatoes and served steaming hot with crusty bread, it's a winner. Just like mum used to make. (Well, apart from the asafetida).

Preparation & cooking time: 40 minutes

Serves: 4 persons

- 3 tablespoons butter
- ¼ teaspoon yellow asafetida powder
- 8-10 medium tomatoes, blanched, peeled and coarsely chopped
- ½ teaspoon brown sugar
- 1½ teaspoons salt
- ½ teaspoon freshly ground black pepper
- ¼ teaspoon dried basil
- 2½ cups light vegetable stock or water, heated
- 1 tablespoon plain flour
- 1 tablespoon chopped fresh parsley

Mum's Tomato Soup

Melt 1 tablespoon butter over low heat in a heavy 3-litre/quart saucepan. When the foam subsides, add the asafetida, tomatoes, sugar, salt, pepper, and basil. Raise the heat to moderate and saute for 2-3 minutes. Stir in the stock or water, raise the heat, bring to a boil, reduce to a simmer, and cook for 15 minutes or until the tomatoes are fully broken down.

Strain the mixture into a large mixing bowl, pressing down on the tomatoes in the strainer to extract as much of the juice as possible. Discard the dry solid residue in the strainer. Set aside the puréed tomatoes. Rinse the saucepan.

Heat the remaining butter in the saucepan over moderate heat. Remove the pan from the heat. With a wooden spoon, stir in the flour to make a smooth paste. Return the pan to the heat and gradually add

the strained tomato mixture, stirring constantly. Bring the mixture to the boil, still stirring.

Stir in the chopped parsley. Turn the soup into a warmed tureen or individual soup bowls and serve hot.

A cool and refreshing soup that can be served as a first course, between courses, or as a dessert. All fruits should be ripe, sweet, and seasonal.

Chilled Summer Fruit Soup

Bring to the boil the apples, grapes, cherries, water, grape juice, pineapple juice, and orange rind in a 4-litre/quart saucepan. Reduce the heat, cover, and simmer for 10 minutes or until the apples are tender. Stir occasionally.

Add the prunes and berries. Continue simmering for about 5 minutes or until the prunes are tender.

Mix the arrowroot with the apple juice until completely dissolved and stir into the soup. Return the soup to a boil and stir constantly for 1 minute, or until the soup thickens. Remove from the heat, add maple syrup (or honey) and orange segments. Chill.

Serve in large soup bowls with a spoonful of sour cream, garnished with a sprig of fresh mint.

Preparation & cooking time: 30 minutes

Serves: 6-8 persons

- 2 small seedless oranges, peeled and cut into small segments
- sour light cream for topping (optional)
- fresh mint sprigs for garnish
- 1 red apple, peeled and cubed
- 2 tablespoons maple syrup or honey
- 250g (9 ounces) green seedless grapes
- 250g (9 ounces) dark sweet cherries, pitted
- 1 cup water
- ½ cup dark grape juice
- ¼ cup pineapple juice
- ¼ teaspoon grated orange rind
- ¼ cup diced, pitted prunes
- 1½ cups berries raspberries, halved strawberries, blueberries, or boysenberries
- 2 teaspoons arrowroot powder
- 1 tablespoon apple juice

U se long-grain rice in this tasty fried combination with sautéed vegetables, tofu, and seasonings. Ideally, the rice should be cooked the day before and cold before frying. The tofu required is the firm rather than the soft or "silken" variety.

Preparation & cooking time: 30 minutes

Serves: 6-8 persons

- 3 tablespoons corn or peanut oil
- 1 teaspoon minced fresh ginger
- ½ teaspoon yellow asafetida powder
- 1 small carrot, cut julienne style
- ¼ cup finely slivered celery
- ¼ cup finely diced cabbage
- ¼ cup unpeeled cucumber pieces, cut match stick-size
- 2 tablespoons bamboo shoots cut match stick-size
- 2 tablespoons diced red pepper
- ¼ cup cooked green peas
- ¼ cup mung bean shoots
- ¼ cup crumbled firm tofu
- 3 tablespoons soy sauce
- 2 teaspoons sesame oil
- 2 teaspoons Chinese chili oil

Savoury Cantonese Fried Rice

- 1 teaspoon salt
- ¼ teaspoon black pepper
- 2 cups long-grain rice, cooked without salt and chilled overnight

Heat 1 tablespoon of the oil in a wok over moderate heat. Sauté the minced ginger in the hot oil for one minute. Add the asafetida, tossing it momentarily with the ginger. Increase the heat to full.

Stir in the carrots, celery, and cabbage and sauté for 2 or 3 minutes. Add the cucumber, bamboo shoots, red peppers, green peas, and bean shoots and sauté for one minute; then add the tofu, soy sauce, sesame oil, chili oil, salt, and pepper. Sauté for another minute.

Empty the contents of the wok into a bowl, cover with a lid, and rinse the wok.

Heat the wok until dry and hot and add the remaining oil. Sauté the chilled long-grain rice in the hot oil over full heat for 3-4 minutes or until hot.

Stir through the vegetables and serve immediately.

Gently toasting the rice in butter, ghee or oil before adding the water, in the style of making risotto, allows all the rice grains to remain separate.

Sautéed Rice with Poppy Seeds

Preparation & cooking time:
30 minutes

Serves: 3 or 4 persons

- 1 cup basmati or other long-grain white rice
- 2 cups water
- ¾ teaspoon salt
- 1 teaspoon fresh lemon juice
- 2-3 tablespoons ghee or oil
- 1½ teaspoons poppy seeds

Bring to the boil the water, salt and lemon juice in a 2-litre/quart saucepan over moderate heat. Keep it covered to avoid evaporation.

Heat the ghee or oil over moderately low heat in a 2-litre/quart saucepan. Sauté the poppy seeds in the hot oil until they become aromatic.

Pour in the boiling water, raise the heat, and allow the water to fully boil for a few seconds, then reduce the heat and allow the rice to gently simmer. Place a tight-fitting lid on the pan and cook without stirring or removing the lid for about 15-20 minutes or until the rice is tender, dry, and fluffy. Turn off the heat, allow the rice to steam another 5 minutes.

Serve hot.

*I*nari-zushi is a popular Japanese takeaway finger food. Slices of deep-fried tofu are opened and used as pouches for sushi rice. They have an intriguing flavour that is at once savoury and sweet. To make them, you will need thin deep-fried tofu slices called 'Inari skin' found in well-stocked Asian supermarkets.

Preparation & cooking time: 30 minutes

Makes: 16 inari-zushi

- 16 pieces thin, Japanese deep-fried tofu slices (known as 'inari skin')
- 3 cups cooked, cooled and seasoned sushi rice (recipe follows)
- 6 teaspoons sesame seeds, dry-roasted in a frying pan until golden
- pickled ginger slices
- soy sauce for dipping

Sushi Rice in Tofu Pouches

Inari-zushi

Prepare the tofu slices: If the inari-skin comes sealed with flavoured juices, drain and use straight from the packet.

Fold the rice with the toasted sesame seeds. Moisten your hands.

Form the rice into 16 golf ball-sized lumps.

Open each tofu pouch by carefully pulling the cut edge apart. Fill each tofu pouch with a ball of rice. Do not fill the pouch too tightly or else it will break. Wrap the edges of the pouch around the rice to form an enclosed pouch. Place onto a serving tray with the folded edge down.

Serve at room temperature accompanied with pickled ginger and soy sauce for dipping.

NOTE: Instead of roasted sesame seeds, try the following alternative flavourings — finely-chopped carrot and lotus root, Japanese pepper *(sansho)*, poppy seeds with finely chopped cucumber, or lemon zest.

Sushi refers to cooked short-grain rice mixed with a sweetened vinegar dressing. It can be topped with a number of vegetarian ingredients, or rolled with different fillings in dark green nori seaweed — the varieties are enormous. As with any rice, it can be successfully cooked in a saucepan or in an electric rice cooker. Any variety of short grain rice will do, although Japanese varieties are particularly appropriate. Makes about 8 cups

Japanese Sushi Rice

Wash and drain the rice.

Place the drained rice and the water, plus the optional kombu, in a heavy bottomed saucepan over moderate heat. Stir until the water boils, reduce to a simmer, cover with a tight-fitting lid, and cook over a very low heat for 15 minutes, or until the rice is cooked and there is no water remaining in the saucepan.

Remove from the heat. Leave the lid on for an additional 10 minutes to allow the rice to firm up. Remove the kombu. Alternatively, place the rice, water and optional kombu in an electric rice cooker, and cook according to manufacturers instructions.

Prepare the vinegar dressing:
Place the vinegar, salt and sugar in a non-reactive saucepan and heat while stirring gently over low heat until the sugar and salt dissolve. Do not boil.

Spread the hot rice out evenly in a large, preferably non-metallic flat-bottomed bowl using a paddle or a wooden spoon.

Pour in the dressing slowly with one hand, gently combining it with the rice while simultaneously fanning the grains with a fan or some newspaper in the other hand. Your aim is to make the rice slightly sticky, with the grains separated and evenly flavoured with the dressing. Continue mixing and fanning until the rice reaches body temperature.

Cover the bowl with a damp cloth. The rice is now ready to be made into sushi.

- **Preparation & cooking time: 30 minutes**
- **Makes: about 8 cups sushi rice**
  - 5 cups short-grain rice, a little more than 1 kilo
  - 5 cups water
  - few pieces kombu (optional)
- **Dressing**
  - 5 tablespoons sushi vinegar
  - 2 tablespoons fine sugar
  - 1 teaspoon salt

*T*hese days it's easy to purchase a ready-mixed combination of baby salad greens from any well-stocked fruit and vegetable supplier. If you prefer to make your own combinations, here's a couple of selections with a tasty herbed oil and lemon dressing, inspired by the traditional niçoise mixture of tiny salad leaves known as mesclun.

Preparation time:
a few minutes

Serves: 4-6 persons

Tender greens selection

- 1 large handful each of baby spinach, metzuma (mizuna), rocket leaves and green oak leaf lettuce leaves

Semi-bitter combination

- ½ small radicchio lettuce
- 1 small bunch rocket leaves (arugula)
- 1 small butter lettuce

Gourmet Green Salad with Herbed French Dressing

Tender greens selection

Combine all the greens. You may like to add watercress, or (lamb's lettuce) as an alternative to, or in conjunction with, the above selection.

Serve with the dressing that follows the next recipe.

Semi-bitter combination

Separate the butter lettuce leaves from their base, and tear them into large pieces. Discard any large stems from the bunch of rocket.

Tear the radicchio leaves into large bite-sized pieces. Combine the salad leaves and serve with the dressing recipe that follows.

Herbed French Dressing

Preparation time: a few minutes

Makes: about ½ cup

- ½ cup extra virgin olive oil
- 2 tablespoons fresh lemon juice
- ¼ teaspoon salt
- ¼ teaspoon freshly-cracked black pepper
- ¼ teaspoon Dijon mustard, or to taste
- 1 teaspoon fresh oregano leaves, chopped
- 1 teaspoon fresh basil leaves, chopped
- 1 teaspoon fresh thyme leaves, chopped
- 2 teaspoons honey

Whisk all the ingredients together until well blended; or combine all the ingredients in a lidded jar and shake vigorously until emulsified.

NOTE: You may like to "jazz-up" the salads with any of the following additions.

- well-chopped toasted walnuts, pecans or hazelnuts
- toasted pine nuts
- halved and seeded black and green grapes
- trimmed and blanched slender asparagus

- tender, ripe, sliced fresh pears
- marinated and sliced artichoke hearts
- kalamata olives
- sliced baby cucumbers
- tender slices of avocado

- blanched bias-cut slices of baby zucchini
- wedges of tender, steamed or oven-roasted baby beetroots
- steamed and julienned baby carrots

- tiny blanched broccoli florets
- slices of fresh fennel root
- blanched snow peas
- slices of roasted red peppers.

If you double the quantities for this rich appetizer and add a rice dish, as well as a salad or soup, you have a delicious substantial meal.

AROUND THE WORLD

Creamy Cauliflower & Snow Peas with Cashews

Heat oil or ghee for deep-frying in a wok or pan over fairly high heat. When the oil is hot, deep-fry the cauliflower pieces in batches, frying them until they can just be pierced with a knife point. Drain the cauliflower pieces, keeping them warm.

Blanch the snow peas in boiling, lightly salted water for 1 minute, or until just tender, and drain them.

Heat 1 teaspoon of olive oil in a frying pan. Sprinkle in the yellow asafetida powder and fry momentarily. Stir-fry the snow peas in the hot oil for 1 minute. Remove from the heat.

Fold in the cauliflower pieces, sour cream, salt, pepper, cashews, sweet chili sauce and coriander leaves.

Serve immediately.

Preparation & cooking time:
25 minutes

Serves: 4 persons

- oil or ghee for deep-frying
- 3 cups cauliflower florets
- 150g (6 ounces) snow peas
- 1 teaspoon olive oil
- ¼ teaspoon yellow asafetida powder
- ½ cup sour cream
- ½ teaspoon salt
- ½ teaspoon freshly-ground black pepper
- ½ cup whole roasted unsalted cashews
- 1 teaspoon sweet chili sauce
- 1 tablespoon chopped fresh coriander leaves

Lightly seasoned fluffy basmati rice makes the best filling for stuffed tomatoes. Be sure to select firm, ripe tomatoes.

Preparation, cooking & baking time: 45-50 minutes

Serves: 6 persons

- 1 cup basmati or other long-grain white rice
- 3 tablespoons ghee or oil
- 6 whole cloves
- one 3.75 cm (1½-inch) cinnamon stick
- 2 whole cardamom pods, bruised
- ⅓ cup slivered almonds
- 2 cups water
- 1 cup fresh green peas
- 1½ teaspoons salt
- 6 large or 12 small firm, ripe tomatoes
- 1½ teaspoons minced fresh ginger
- ½ teaspoon turmeric

Baked Tomatoes Stuffed with Rice and Green Peas

Prepare the rice filling:

Slowly bring to the boil the water, salt and peas to a boil in a covered pan.

Heat 2 tablespoons ghee or oil in a heavy 2-litre/quart saucepan over moderate heat. When the ghee is hot, add the whole cloves, cinnamon stick, bruised cardamom pods, and almonds. Stir-fry for 30 seconds or until the almonds are golden. Add the rice to the spice and nut mixture and stir-fry for about 2 minutes or until the rice is whitish.

Add the boiling water to the rice and nut mixture. Stir, raising the heat to high and bringing the water to a full boil. Immediately reduce the heat to low, cover with a tight-fitting lid and, without stirring, simmer for 15 to 20 minutes or until the rice is dry and tender. Fluff the rice with a fork and (if desired) remove the whole spices.

Stuff and bake the tomatoes:

Preheat the oven to 180°C/355°F.

Cut a thin slice off the top of each tomato and set the slices aside. With a teaspoon, scoop out the seeds and pulp, leaving a 0.5 cm (¼-inch) thick case, and set them aside. Chop or blend the tomato pulp and force it through a strainer. Collect the pulp and discard the seeds.

Heat 1 tablespoon ghee or oil in a 1-litre/quart saucepan over medium heat. When hot, drop in the minced ginger and fry until brown. Add the tomato pulp, ½ teaspoon salt, and turmeric and cook for 5 minutes or until the pulp is reduced to a thick purée.

Stuff the tomatoes with the savoury rice filling and pour a teaspoon of the thick tomato sauce into the opening of each tomato. Replace the tops of the tomatoes.

Bake the tomatoes in a casserole dish in the oven at 180°C/360°F for 10 or 15 minutes.

Serve hot.

Most people associate maple syrup with pancakes, waffles, ice-cream or puddings. Here it plays a part in a savoury context, as a main player in a marinade for crusty pan-fried panir steaks.

Preparation & cooking time: about 1 hour

Serves: 6 persons

- 2 tablespoons olive oil
- ½ teaspoon yellow asafetida powder
- 6 panir steaks (recipe follows)
- sweet potato mash to serve (recipe follows)
- rocket salad to serve (recipe follows)

Marinade

- 3 tablespoons maple syrup
- ¼ teaspoon cayenne pepper
- 1 tablespoon tomato paste
- 1 tablespoon soy sauce
- 1 tablespoon dijon or seed mustard
- 2 tablespoons lemon juice
- 3 tablespoons water

Panir Steaks with Maple Syrup Marinade, Sweet Potato Mash & Rocket Salad

Whisk together all the marinade ingredients in a bowl.

Heat the olive oil in a ridged grill pan placed over fairly high heat.

Sprinkle in the yellow asafetida powder and fry momentarily.

Fry the panir steaks in the flavoured oil on both sides until crusty, then pour over the marinade. Cook the panir steaks, turning until the liquid is slightly reduced, then remove from the heat.

Serve the panir steaks on sweet potato mash with any pan juices poured over, accompanied by the rocket salad.

Rocket Salad

- 1 tablespoon olive oil
- 1 tablespoon lemon juice
- salt and pepper to taste
- 100g (4 ounces) rocket leaves

Whisk the olive oil, lemon juice, salt and pepper.

Pour over the rocket leaves.

Sweet Potato Mash

- 1 kg (2 pounds) orange or white sweet-potato, sliced thick
- 2 tablespoons melted butter, or more to taste
- 1 teaspoon salt
- ½ teaspoon freshly-ground black pepper

Boil the sweet potato in salted water until tender. Drain.

Mash thoroughly and mix in the butter, salt and black pepper.

Panir Steaks

- 5 litres/quarts fresh milk
- 3-4 cups yogurt or 6-8 tablespoons lemon juice

Heat the milk to boiling point in a heavy-based saucepan.

Stir in three-quarters of the yogurt or lemon juice. The milk should separate into chunky curds, leaving a greenish liquid residue called whey. If not completely separated, add a little more yogurt or lemon juice. Drape a double thickness of cheesecloth over a colander placed in the sink.

Scoop out the curds with a slotted spoon and place them in the cheesecloth. Pour the whey, along with remaining curds in the saucepan, into the cheesecloth. Gather the ends of the cloth together and hold the bag of curd cheese under cold running water for 30 seconds. Twist the bag tightly to squeeze out extra whey, return it to the colander.

Press under a heavy weight for 10-15 minutes. Carefully remove the curd cheese from the cloth. Your panir is ready. Slice into 6 steaks.

*M*illet is a light, versatile and inviting grain with a mild, nutty taste, distinctive without being unusual. To bring out the flavour in millet, the tiny yellow grains are toasted in butter or oil before cooking in stock or water. Millet is a thirsty grain, so serve this pilaff alongside a juicy vegetable dish or soup.

Preparation & cooking time: 35-40 minutes

Serves: 6 persons

- 2½ cups water or vegetable stock
- ½ cup frozen corn kernels
- 1 cup tomatoes, diced fine
- 1 teaspoon salt
- ¼ teaspoon black pepper
- 2 tablespoons butter, olive oil, or a combination
- 1 teaspoon yellow asafetida powder
- 2 teaspoons julienned fresh ginger root
- 2 small green chilies, seeded and chopped
- ¾ cup diced red capsicums (peppers)
- 1¼ cups hulled millet
- ¼ cup toasted pine nuts

Millet Pilaff with Corn, Peppers & Pine Nuts

Combine the stock, corn, tomato, salt and pepper in a small saucepan. Bring to a boil and simmer, fully covered, over low heat.

Heat the oil or butter in a saucepan over moderate heat. Add the yellow asafetida powder, the ginger, chili, green capsicum and the millet.

Pan-fry the millet for 3-4 inutes, or until it darkens a few shades.

Pour the simmering stock into the toasted grains, bring to the boil, reduce the heat to low, cover, and cook for about 20 minutes, or until the liquid has been absorbed and the grains are soft. Set aside for 5 minutes to firm up.

Serve hot with a sprinkle of toasted pine nuts.

*C*hutney varies immensely according to the kind of apples used, but invariably sour Granny Smiths seem to produce the best results. This chutney is hot yet sweet and can be served as an accompaniment to a great variety of savoury dishes. Allow 1-4 spoonfuls per serving. Apple chutney can be refrigerated in a sealed container.

Hot 'n' Spicy Apple Chutney

Heat the ghee or oil in a heavy 2-litre/quart saucepan over medium heat. Sauté the cumin seeds in the hot ghee until golden brown. Add the green chilies and minced ginger and sauté for 1 minute; then add the turmeric and the sliced apples. Stir-fry for 2-3 minutes.

Reduce the heat to low and add the water, cinnamon, and nutmeg. Cook, stirring occasionally, for about 15-20 minutes or until the apples become soft.

Add the sugar and continue to cook the chutney until it becomes jam-like.

Serve at room temperature or cover and refrigerate for up to a week.

Preparation & cooking time: 1 hour

Serves: 10 persons

- 2 tablespoons ghee or oil
- 1½ teaspoons cumin seeds
- 2 fresh hot green chilies cut into thin rings
- 2 teaspoons minced fresh ginger
- 1 teaspoon turmeric
- 500g (about 1 pound) tangy green apples, peeled, cored and sliced
- ¼ cup water
- 1¼ teaspoons ground cinnamon
- ¾ teaspoon ground nutmeg
- 1 cup sugar

*A*lthough it may seem an unlikely combination, herbed potato mixed with feta cheese and fried in crispy spring roll wrappers really does work incredibly well. And as far as the super-quick, super-quirky green pea chutney goes, that's also surprisingly delicious.

Preparation & cooking time: about 40 minutes

Serves: 46 persons

- 600g (1¼ pounds) potatoes, peeled and cut into large chunks
- 4 tablespoons butter
- 200g (7 ounces) feta cheese, cut into tiny cubes
- ½-1 teaspoon salt, depending on the saltiness of the feta
- 1 teaspoon freshly-ground black pepper
- 1-2 tablespoons fresh mint, coriander or parsley, chopped
- 16 spring roll wrappers
- 1 teaspoon cornflour (cornstarch), made into a paste with a little cold water
- oil for deep-frying
- green pea chutney to serve (recipe follows)

Feta & Potato Spring Rolls with Green Pea Chutney

Boil the potatoes in lightly salted water until soft. Mash them thoroughly with the butter, and fold in the feta, salt, pepper and herbs.

Divide the mixture into 16, and roll each portion into a log about 12cm (4½ inches) long. Place a log near the corner of a spring roll sheet.

Roll the sheet over the filling, tuck in the sides and roll up tightly. Seal the final corner with a dab of paste. Continue filling the remaining spring rolls. Heat the oil over moderate heat until fairly hot.

Deep-fry the spring rolls, turning once, for about 45 seconds or until lightly browned. Drain on paper towels.

Serve hot or warm with the green pea chutney.

Green Pea Chutney

Makes: about 1¼ cups

- ⅓ cup almonds, pan-toasted until golden, and chopped
- 1 cup frozen peas, defrosted
- 1 teaspoon grated fresh ginger
- 2-3 tablespoons water
- 2 teaspoons fresh lime juice
- ¼ cup fresh coriander leaves
- 1 teaspoon salt
- ½ teaspoon freshly-ground pepper

Pulse the toasted almonds in a food processor until finely minced.

Add the remaining ingredients and process until smooth. If you prefer a looser consistency, add a little more water and pulse again.

Serve with the spring rolls.

*T*urkish breads, pide, make a soft and inviting pizza base. The recipe here has some of my favourite toppings — or try some of the alternative varieties suggested below.

Quick Turkish Bread Pizza

The sauce:

Heat the olive oil in a saucepan over moderate heat. Sprinkle in the yellow asafetida powder, fry momentarily, add the rest of the ingredients and cook uncovered for 10-15 minutes or until fairly thick. Cool.

Assemble the pizza:

Spread the sauce over the bread. Sprinkle with half the cheese, the remaining topping ingredients, and then the rest of the cheese.

Bake in a preheated 220°C/430°F oven for about 10 minutes or until the cheese is melted and bubbling.

Serve either warm or hot.

Some more pizza ideas

- Artichoke hearts, sundried tomatoes, bocconcini, rocket pesto and Parmesan
- Pan-fried fresh fennel root with sundried tomatoes and fresh oregano.
- Tri-coloured grilled peppers with cherry tomatoes, olives and fresh bocconcini
- Baby spinach, cottage cheese, semi-dried tomatoes, pine nuts and Parmesan
- Potato with rosemary leaves
- Asparagus with pine nut pesto, sun dried capsicum and mozzarella
- Sweet potato, oven-dried tomato halves, grilled baby eggplants, goat's cheese, olives and fresh oregano
- Pizza primavera — tender broccoli florets, grilled zucchini and red peppers, asparagus, mozzarella, cheddar, roma tomatoes and Parmesan.

Preparation & cooking time:
35 - 40 minutes

Makes: one 25cm (10-inch) pizza

Sauce

- 1½ tablespoons olive oil
- ½ teaspoon yellow asafetida powder
- 1½ cups tomato purée
- 1 tablespoon tomato paste
- ½ teaspoon each dried basil and oregano
- 1 teaspoon sugar
- 1 teaspoon salt
- ½ teaspoon freshly-ground black pepper

Topping

- 150g (5 ounces) fresh buffalo mozzarella, chopped coarsely
- 2 tablespoons grated Parmesan cheese
- 1 small eggplant, sliced into rings and fried
- 1 small red capsicum (pepper), grilled peeled and sliced
- 1 small yellow capsicum (pepper), grilled peeled and sliced
- ⅓ cup kalamata olives, pitted and halved
- sprinkle dried oregano
- one 25cm (10-inch) Turkish bread

Succulent stewed dried fruits couple wonderfully with the ubiquitous Middle Eastern rice flour pudding known as muhallabeya.

Winter Fruit Compote with Fragrant Syrian Milk Pudding

**Dried fruit soaking time:
1 hour**

**Preparation & cooking time:
40-45 minutes**

Serves: 6 persons

- 300g (11 ounces) dried figs
- 1 cup sugar
- 1 vanilla bean, split
- 1 cinnamon stick
- fine zest from 1 orange and ½ lemon
- juice from 1 orange and half lemon
- 150g (5 ounces) pitted prunes
- 100g (4 ounces) dried apricots
- 200g (7 ounces) dried peaches

Soak the figs in hot water for 1 hour. Drain.

Combine the sugar, vanilla bean, cinnamon stick, zest and citrus juice in a saucepan, along with 1½ cups of water.

Bring to a boil, reduce the heat and simmer for 10 minutes. Add the dried figs along with the rest of the dried fruits, and simmer with a tightly fitting lid for ½ hour or until the fruits are tender. Cool to room temperature.

Serve with the fragrant milk pudding.

*M*ake sure you have a whisk on hand — there's some serious whiskin' ahead.

Fragrant Syrian Milk Pudding

Whisk the rice flour with a cup of the cold milk, adding it gradually and mixing thoroughly to avoid lumps.

Bring to the boil the rest of the milk in your heaviest pan.

Whisk in the rice flour and milk mixture, stirring vigorously. Cook on very low heat, stirring continuously for 10-15 minutes, or until the mixture thickens. Whisk in the sugar until dissolved then remove the saucepan from the heat and pour in the rosewater.

Whisk the whole mixture until creamy smooth, and chill.

Serve: Transfer the pudding to a large serving bowl, or individual ones, and sprinkle with the chopped pistachio nuts. Serve as an accompaniment to the fruit compote.

Preparation & cooking time: 20 - 25 minutes

Serves: 6 persons

- scant 1¼ cups rice flour
- 1.2 litres (2 pints) cold milk
- ½ cup sugar
- 1-2 tablespoons pure distilled rosewater
- 1-2 tablespoons chopped pistachio nuts

Every community has its own traditional flavourings and presentation for muhallabeya, some flavouring it with orange blossom water, or rosewater, and sprinkling it with chopped almonds or pistachios. The Turkish version uses vanilla or lemon zest, whereas the Iranians prefer cardamom.

Glossary

AJOWAN SEEDS
Tiny, light-brown spice seeds closely related to caraway and cumin. They have a slightly hot, semi-bitter thyme-like flavour, and are used in many North Indian savoury dishes, especially in fried snacks. Ajowan seeds, *Carum ajowan,* also known as *omum,* bishop's weed, and *ajwain,* aid digestion and are used to relieve stomach problems. As well as being a culinary flavouring, they are cultivated for their essential oil, thymol. The seeds keep indefinitely and are available from Indian and Middle Eastern grocers.

ANISE SEEDS
Highly aromatic seeds of the annual herb *Pimpinella anisum.* These greenish-grey, slightly crescent-shaped seeds have a very strong licorice-like flavour and odour, although they are not related to the perennial plant of the pea family whose sweet roots are the source of true licorice. Anise is generally used as flavouring for drinks, sweets, creams, and breads such as pumpernickel. Anise seeds are available at supermarkets and specialty stores.

ARUGULA
Also known as roquette, *ruccola,* rocket and *rughetta.* A small, green, leafy plant resembling radish tops that grows wild in the Mediterranean region. When purchasing or harvesting arugula, choose young plants with small, slender, dark green leaves. *Arugula* is related to mustard, and has a peppery, slightly bitter, slightly acidic flavour. It is used as one of the ingredients of mesclun, the traditional Niçoise mixture of tiny salad leaves.

ASAFETIDA
The aromatic resin from the root of the giant fennel, *Ferula asafoetida.* Asafetida, also known as hing, is extracted from the stems of these giant perennial plants that grow wild in Central Asia. In the spring, when the plant is about to bloom, the stems and roots are cut. Milky resin exudes from the cut surface and is scraped off. The gummy resin is sun-dried into a solid mass that is then sold in solid, wax-like pieces, or, more conveniently, in powdered form. Asafetida has been held in great esteem among indigenous medicines from the earliest times in India. It is highly reputed as a drug that expels wind from the stomach and counteracts spasmodic disorders. It is also a digestive agent and is used, among other things, for alleviating toothache and as an antidote for opium.

Due to the presence of sulphur compounds, raw asafetida has a distinctive pungent aroma. To cook with asafetida, small quantities of the powdered form are sautéed in a little slightly hot oil or ghee, before adding to a variety of savoury dishes, adding a delicious flavour reminiscent of a mixture of shallots and garlic.

I always use the mild yellow asafetida powder and not the grey variety. All recipes for this book using asafetida were tested using this yellow variety. If using other types, reduce the quantity to somewhere between a quarter and a half of the suggested amount. Asafetida is available at Indian grocers and specialty stores.

ATTA FLOUR
Also known as *chapati* flour, this low-gluten flour is derived from a strain of soft wheat popular throughout India. The entire wheat kernel, including the bran, germ and endosperm, is ground very finely, making a nutritious flour. *Atta* flour is suitable for all Indian flatbreads, such as *poories, chapatis,* and parathas. Doughs made from atta flour are velvety smooth, knead readily and respond easily to shaping and rolling. *Atta* flour is available from Indian and Asian grocery stores.

AYURVEDA
Ancient India's great medical treatise. The word Ayurveda literally means 'the science of healthful living', and remains as the world's oldest known work on biology, botany, herbology, anatomy, hygiene, medicine, surgery and nutrition.

BALSAMIC VINEGAR
A highly fragrant, sweetish vinegar from Italy made from concentrated grape juice and aged in wood for at least 10 years.

BANGKWANG
(See **YAM BEAN**.)

BARLEY FLOUR
Coarsely ground barley flour is used

as a bread ingredient in European cuisine, notably in German *pumpernickel.* Wholegrain barley flour has a nutty flavour, with its colour darker and a texture coarser than wheat flour. You can replace up to one-third of the wheat flour in baked products with barley flour, although you will have to adjust the quantity of liquid as it absorbs more water than wheat flour. It is available from health food stores and many well-stocked supermarkets.

BASIL

The fragrant aromatic herb, *Ocimum basilicum*, known also as sweet basil. It is a small, profusely branched, bushy plant, whose tender green leaves are used worldwide, especially in Italian cuisine, where it is used mostly in dishes containing tomatoes and in salads and soups, on pizzas and in pasta dishes. There are many types of basil, which vary in size, colour and flavour, and all can be used for culinary purposes. Greek basil, purple ruffle, and dark opal are three useful varieties. (See also **THAI BASIL**.)

BASMATI RICE

A superb, light-textured, long-grained aromatic rice from North India and Pakistan, with a wonderful fragrance and flavour. Even served plain with a little ghee or butter, *basmati* rice is a treat. I have found Dehradun *basmati* to be most superior in taste and texture. *Basmati* rice is easy to cook and although more costly than other long-grained rices, it is well worth the extra expense. *Basmati* rice is

available at Indian, Middle Eastern and Asian grocers.

BAY LEAVES

The leaves of the sweet bay or laurel tree, *Laurus nobilis,* an evergreen member of the laurel family native to the Mediterranean region and Asia Minor. The highly aromatic leaves are thick, dark green and glossy on the upper surface. Bay leaves used in their fresh or dried form are quite pungent with a slightly bitter, spicy flavour. They are popular in French cuisine.

BESAN
(See **CHICKPEA FLOUR**)

BLACK BEANS

These shiny, black kidney-shaped beans, are also known as Turtle beans. They are a variety of kidney beans, *Phaseolus vulgaris*. They are good source of vegetable protein and exceptionally rich in dietary fibre. Available from Latin American and Asian grocers.

BLACK CUMIN SEEDS

Known as *shahi* or *siyah jeera*, it is the spice seed of a wild annual plant, *Cuminum nigrum,* which grows profusely in North India's mountainous regions. They are often confused with *nigella* or *kalonji,* which are teardrop shaped. Black cumin seeds, however, are darker and thinner than cumin seeds. They are exclusively used in North Indian cuisine, especially in Kashmir. They're available at well-stocked Indian grocers.

BLACK PEPPER
(See **PEPPER**)

BLACK SALT

A reddish-grey variety of salt with a distinct ìhard-boiled eggî flavour. Black salt, or *kala namak* as it is known in Indian cuisine, is a major ingredient in the spice-blend *chat masala*. It is available at Indian grocers.

BOCCONCINI

A fresh, Italian mild-flavoured cheese, a little like mozzarella. It is hand-moulded into creamy white balls and sold swimming in whey. Ideally, it should be eaten as soon as possible after buying. If unavailable, fresh Italian mozzarella made from the milk of water buffaloes (*mozzarella di buffala*) is an excellent alternative.

BOK CHOY

The common Cantonese name for Chinese cabbage. These small cabbages used in Chinese cooking have dark green leaves and wide, white stalks joined near the base of the stem. They resemble a miniature Swiss chard (silverbeet). The smaller the individual cabbage, the more delicate the flavour. Bok choy is available at Chinese grocers.

BROAD BEANS

Also known as *fava* beans in Italy, *haba* in Spanish cuisines and *ful nabed* in the Middle East. Green broad bean pods can be picked young and the beans removed and cooked and eaten fresh. If left on the plant to ripen, the pods will dry out.

Then the dried beans can be removed and stored until required. Whole dried beans must be soaked and the skins removed before cooking. Available at Continental, Spanish, or Middle Eastern grocers.

BUTTERMILK

Real buttermilk is the liquid residue after cream has been churned into butter. However, the buttermilk referred to here and used in this book is cultured buttermilk, which is low-fat milk cultured in a similar way to yoghurt to produce a pleasant, mild-tasting dairy product, with the consistency of light cream. Available at most well-stocked supermarkets.

CANDLE NUTS

These tropical nuts are so oily they can be burned like a candle, hence the name. Under the name of *kemiri* or *burah keras,* they are used in Malay and Indonesian cooking, crushed in soups, and ground with other ingredients. Candle nuts are available from Asian grocers. If they're hard to track down, macadamia nuts are a good substitute.

CARAWAY

Caraway seeds are the fruits of the hardy biennial herb, *Carum carvi,* a native of Europe, Asia and North Africa. The brown seeds are curved and tapered at one end, and are sometimes mistaken for cumin seeds, although they taste quite different. Caraway seeds are warm, sweet, biting and pleasantly acrid. They are a favourite flavouring for many kinds of rye bread and are also widely used in cheese, cakes and biscuits.

CARDAMOM

The aromatic seeds of the fruit of the tropical plant *Elettaria cardamomum,* a member of the ginger family that grows in the moist, tropical regions of South India and Sri Lanka. Cardamom is the world's third-most costly spice, topped only by saffron and vanilla.

The odour and flavour of cardamom is quite pronounced, reminiscent of lemon rind and eucalyptus. Cardamom is popular in some Middle Eastern dishes. In Indian cuisine, cardamom is used in rice dishes, milk sweets and halava. It is also chewed as a breath freshener and digestive aid after a meal.

Cardamom is available in the pod (green or bleached) as decorticated seeds (the outer shell having been removed) or powdered. I would suggest you shun the latter forms and purchase whole pods, available at Indian and Middle Eastern grocery stores for the freshest and most flavoursome cardamom experience.

CASSIA
(See **CINNAMON**)

CAMPHOR

A pure white crystalline powder derived from steam of the camphor tree, Cinnamomum camphera, which in China and India. It is used in tiny amounts to flavour at some Indian grocers and pharmacies. Indian milk sweets and puddings.

CHILI OIL

A fiery hot oil used in Chinese cooking. To make your own chili oil, stir-fry 3 or 4 dried red chilies in a few tablespoons of oil over moderate heat for 3 minutes. Strain the oil and use as required. Alternatively, chili oil can be purchased at any Chinese or South East Asian grocer.

CAPERS

The pickled flour buds of the wild Mediterranean bush *Capparis rupestris*. Capers have been used as a condiment for thousands of years, and they feature especially in French and Italian cuisine. They have a distinct sour, salty flavour.

CAYENNE PEPPER

The orange-red to deep-red powder derived from small, sun-dried, pungent red chili peppers (*Capsicum frutescens*). This bitingly hot condiment should be used with restraint, for a small amount will add considerable zest and flavour to dishes. It is used in a number of hot dishes, notably in Mexican and Indian cuisine. Cayenne is available from supermarkets or well-stocked grocers.

CHANA DAL

Husked, split whole dried brown chickpeas (a relative of the common chickpea). They are very popular in Indian cuisine, especially in *dal* dishes and savouries, being tasty, nutritious, and easy to digest. Chana *dal* is roasted and ground into chickpea flour *(besan),* and used throughout India for savouries and sweets. (See also **CHICKPEA FLOUR**)

CHAPATI FLOUR
(See **ATTA FLOUR**)

CHAT MASALA
A traditional companion to freshly cut fruit in Indian cuisine. This light-brown spice blend contains a number of ingredients, notably black salt, mango powder and asafetida. Sprinkled on fruit with a few drops of fresh lime juice, it makes a deliciously different dessert. Available from Indian grocery stores.

CHICKPEA FLOUR
The finely milled, pale-yellow flour from ground, roasted chana *dal*. It is popular in Indian cuisine for making batter, as a binding agent, and in confectionery. It is also known as besan flour, gram flour and peas meal, and is available at Indian grocers. (See also **CHANA DAL**)

CHICKPEAS
Known as *garbanzos* in Spanish-speaking countries or *ceci* in Italy, chickpeas are the peas from the pods of the plant *Cicer arietimum*. They are popular in India in their immature, green state, whereas they are commonly known outside of India in their dried state. These large, light-brown wrinkled peas must be soaked before use, then boiled until soft. They are used extensively in many cuisines around the world, especially Indian, Mexican and Middle Eastern. They

are rich in protein - 100g (3¼ ounces) of cooked chickpeas contain 20g of protein. Chickpeas provide nearly double the amount of iron and more vitamin C than most legumes. Chickpeas are available at Continental, Indian and Middle Eastern grocers and at well-stocked supermarkets.

CHILIES
Chilies, sweet and hot, are members of *Solanaceae,* a vast assemblage of plants to which potato, tomato and eggplant also belong. All chilies fall into the category of *Capsicum* and most of the readily available ones belong to the *annuum* species. There are hundreds of varieties of chilies, over 150 in Mexico alone, ranging in potency from sweet to fiery hot. The chemical in chilies that gives them heat and therapeutic value is capsacin. The more *capsacin* a chili contains, the hotter it is. The seeds and the inner white ribs are the hottest part and often a recipe calls for removing both to tame the heat.

CHOY SUM
This plant is grown in various parts of the world, and is used extensively in Chinese and Japanese cuisine as a vegetable. It is delicately flavoured, with yellow flowers, succulent green stalks, and small bright green leaves branching from a central stem. This attractive vegetable is available from Chinese grocers all year around.

CINNAMON
Cinnamomum zeylanicum is a moderate-sized, bushy evergreen tree of

the laurel family, whose dried inner bark is true cinnamon. Native to Southern India and Sri Lanka, the thin, bark sheaths are sundried and packed, one inside the other, to produce "sticks" or "quills".

Confusion sometimes exists in distinguishing cinnamon from cassia. In some countries, what is sold as cinnamon is in fact cassia (*Cinnamomum cassia*). Cassia is a taller tree with smaller flowers and fruits than true cinnamon. In general, Cassia is prepared for the market in much the same way as cinnamon, and their flavours are similar, although cinnamon is less pungent and more delicate than cassia. Cassia powder is reddish-brown, while cinnamon powder is tan. Cinnamon or cassia sticks impart a sweet, aromatic flavour to fancy Indian rice dishes, vegetables and dals. Ground to a powder, cinnamon is an important ingredient in the North Indian spice blend *garam masala*. Cinnamon also features extensively in Middle Eastern and European cuisine. It is available at supermarkets and Indian and Middle Eastern grocers.

CLOVES
The dried nail-shaped buds from a neat evergreen tree with aromatic pink buds. These buds, when hand-picked and dried, turn a reddish-brown to become the cloves with which we are familiar.

Good cloves should have a strong, pungent, sweet aroma and flavour and should be well-formed, plump and oily. Cloves have diverse uses in different cuisines of the world, being used for cakes, tarts and pastries, fancy rice dishes, soup stocks, sweet cooked fruits and in various spice blends, including some North Indian garam masalas. Cloves are available at supermarkets and Indian grocery stores.

COCONUT

The coconut palm, *Cocos nucifera,* is grown on tropical coasts all over the world and is the source of many products. Most important are the nuts (technically called drupes). When coconuts are picked green, one can extract their sweet juice as a beverage. The pulp inside is used in many South Indian savoury dishes. When coconuts ripen on the tree, the picked fruits yield moist, white "meat", which is excellent in varieties of vegetable dishes, savouries, rice dishes, sweets, chutneys and beverages, especially in Indian and South-East Asian cuisine.

Dried coconut is desiccated and is familiar in Western cuisine as an ingredient in sweets and cakes. When a recipe calls for fresh coconut, however, dried desiccated coconut is a poor substitute. Fresh coconuts are easily available in tropical areas and can even be found for sale far from their place of origin. They will be suitable as long as they are still full of juice and have no cracks or signs of mould around their "eyes". Once cracked open, separated from their husk and peeled, fresh coconut can be sliced, grated, shredded, stored in the refrigerator for several days or frozen.

COCONUT MILK

Known as *santan* in Indonesian cooking, this creamy white liquid with a fresh coconut flavour is extracted from fresh coconut pulp and is used in varieties of South-East Asian and Indonesian dishes. It is available in cans from supermarkets and Asian grocers.

CONTINENTAL PARSLEY
(See **PARSLEY**)

CORIANDER LEAVES

The fresh leaves of the hardy annual plant *Coriandrum sativum,* fresh coriander is one of the most commonly used flavouring herbs in the world, certainly on par with parsley. It is found in markets throughout the Middle East, China, South-East Asia, India and South and Central America. Bunches of coriander can be recognised by their smell and their fan-like lower leaves and feathery upper ones.

Also known as *cilantro,* Chinese parsley and *har dhania,* fresh coriander is a zesty and delicious addition to many of the worldís cuisines. Its unique, warm-bodied taste is found in Indian vegetable dishes, dals, savories and fresh chutneys. It also makes a very beautiful garnish. Purchase fresh coriander from oriental and Latin American grocers or well-stocked produce markets and greengrocers.

CORIANDER SEEDS

The seeds of the annual herb *Coriandrum sativum.* Coriander seeds are a favourite flavouring spice in Indian, Cypriot and some Latin American cuisines. They are almost round, brown to yellowish-red, with a warm, distinctive fragrance and a pleasant taste, mild and sweet and yet slightly pungent, reminiscent of a combination of sage and lemon. Coriander is available whole or ground, although I recommend obtaining the whole seeds and grinding them yourself when you need the freshest coriander flavour. Known as dhania in Indian cuisine, coriander complements the flavour of many savoury dishes. Coriander seeds are available at Indian and Middle Eastern grocery stores and well-stocked supermarkets.

CORNFLOUR

When I mention cornflour in this book, I am referring to what Americans call "cornstarch", and not to the flour milled from corn. Cornflour, sometimes referred to as wheat starch, is the dry white powdered starch remaining when the proteins have been removed from wheat flour. It is used in many cuisines, especially Chinese, as a thickener for sauces. It is available from any grocer or supermarket.

CORN MEAL
(See **POLENTA**)

COUSCOUS

A grain product made from semolina. It is also the name of the famous dish of which couscous is the main ingredient, being one of the most common and widely known North African Arab dishes. Available at well-stocked supermarkets and Middle Eastern grocers.

CUMIN SEEDS

The seeds of the small annual herb of the parsley family, *Cuminum cyminum*. Cumin seeds are oval and yellowish-brown, similar in appearance to the caraway seeds, but longer. They have a warm, strongly aromatic and slightly bitter flavour and are used extensively in Indian, Middle Eastern and Latin American cuisines (especially in Mexican dishes).

The flavour and aroma of cumin, like most spice seeds, emerges best after they have been dry-roasted or added to hot oil. In Indian cuisine, cumin is popular in vegetable dishes, yogurt-based salads, raitas, *dals,* and savouries. Cumin seeds can be obtained from any Indian or Middle Eastern grocer, or well-stocked supermarkets.

CURD CHEESE

The simplest type of unripened fresh cheese, produced by adding an acidic curdling agent to boiled raw milk. This versatile food ingredient is popular in all varieties of Indian cuisine, where it is known as *panir* and it can also be used as a substitute for tofu, feta or farmer's cheese. It is high in protein, has a soft consistency, and is sweeter and creamier than tofu. It can be cubed and deep-fried, and added to moist

vegetable dishes and rice dishes, crumbled into salads, kneaded and rolled into small balls, and made into confectionery.

(TO) CURDLE

When small amounts of acidic substances are added to hot milk, a protein known as casein coagulates and forms solid lumps known commonly as curd. Other proteins, principal among them lacto-globulin, remain suspended in the liquid, known as whey.

CURRY LEAVES

The thin, shiny, dark-green leaves of the South East Asian tree *Murraya koenigii.* Curry leaves are highly aromatic when fresh. Used especially in South Indian kitchens, they are generally sautéed in oil with mustard seeds and asafetida and added to dals, fresh coconut chutney or vegetable dishes. They are an important ingredient in one variety of curry powder used in Tamil Nadu. Dried leaves are inferior, but sometimes that is all that is available. Obtain curry leaves from Indian grocery stores.

DAL

A generic name for all members of the dried pea and bean family, and also the name of the thick, gravy-like or thin soup-like dishes made from them. *Dal,* besides being a good source of iron and B vitamins, is an excellent source of vegetable protein.

(TO) DRY ROAST

This technique refers to the process

of slowly browning whole spice seeds, split dal, nuts and seeds and some types of flour. It is best done in a heavy pan or griddle that has been pre-warmed over low heat. The ingredients are stir-fried, without the addition of any oil or liquid, until lightly browned, releasing flavourful volatile oils and aromatic fragrances.

FENNEL

The tall, hardy, aromatic perennial of the parsley family native to southern Europe and the Mediterranean area. Fennel *(Foeniculum vulgare)* is distinguished by its finely divided, feathery green foliage and its golden-yellow flowers. It is used both as a herb and for its aromatic seeds. In Italian cuisine, the bulb of the Florence fennel, or *finocchio,* is used whole, sliced, or quartered as a vegetable and either braised or baked au gratin. It is also chopped raw in salads. Wild fennel stems and the frondy leaves, with a slightly bitter anise taste, are used in cooking, especially to flavour sauces. Fennel seeds, although used to some extent in European cooking, are especially favoured in Indian cuisine. The oval, greenish or yellowish-brown seeds have an agreeable, warm, sweet fragrance, similar to that of anise. Fennel seeds appear in Kashmiri and Punjabi dishes and are one of the five spices in the Bengali spice blend called *panch puran.* They are used in a variety of vegetable dishes, *dals* and pastries. The most common use of fennel seeds in Indian cuisine is as an after-dinner digestive. They are dry-roasted, and chewed, freshening the breath and stimulating digestion. Fresh fennel bulbs are available seasonally at good greengrocer shops. The seeds are available at Indian grocers.

FENUGREEK

An erect annual herb of the bean family, indigenous to western Asia and south-eastern Europe. Fenugreek *(Trigonella foenum-graecum)* is cultivated for its seeds, which, although legumes, are used as a spice.

The seeds are small, hard, yellowish-brown, smooth and oblong, with a little groove across one corner. Fenugreek has a warm, slightly bitter taste, reminiscent of burnt sugar and maple. The seeds are used in Greece and Egypt and especially India, where they are lightly dry-roasted or fried to extract their characteristic flavour. One should note, however, that over-roasting or over-frying fenugreek results in an excessive bitter taste. The leaves of the fenugreek plant are also popular in Indian cuisine. Known as *methi,* they are used in vegetable dishes, breads and savories. Easily home-grown, fresh young fenugreek leaves are wonderful in salads, dressed with oil and lemon. Fenugreek seeds are available at Indian or Middle Eastern grocers. The fresh leaves (if you are shopping outside India), can occasionally be found in markets or can be home-grown.

FINOCCHIO
(See **FENNEL**)

FILO PASTRY

A very light and paper-thin pastry popular throughout the Middle East and in Greece. This delicate pastry is used for either sweet or savoury dishes. Filo is difficult to prepare at home and is best purchased refrigerated from well-stocked supermarkets, delicatessens, and health food stores.

FIVE SPICE

Two varieties of five spice are prominent in the world of vegetarian cuisine: Chinese five spice powder and Indian *panch puran,* a blend of five whole spices. Chinese five spice powder is a combination of five dried, ground spices, generally cinnamon, cloves, fennel, star anise and Sichuan peppercorns, the pungent, brown peppercorns native to the Sichuan province.

When used as a condiment for fried food, it is used in sparing quantities because it is very potent. Try making your own by grinding together two or three small sections of cinnamon stick, a dozen cloves, two teaspoons of fennel seeds, two teaspoons of Sichuan peppercorns and three or four star anise. Keep the powder in a well-sealed jar in a cool, dry place. Obtain your ingredients at any Asian grocery store. You can also purchase Chinese five spice ready-made.

Panch puran is most often associated with Bengali cuisine. It is a combination of equal quantities of fenugreek seeds, cumin seeds, fennel seeds, black mustard seeds and *nigella (kalonji)* seeds. Panch puran is always fried in ghee or oil before use to release the dormant flavour in the seeds. Mix your own, or purchase it ready-made at Indian grocery stores.

GALANGAL

There are two varieties of *galangal* greater and lesser. Both are closely related, although the lesser is more important. Greater *galangal (Alpinia galanga),* native to Indonesia, is related to ginger. Its large, knobbly, spicy roots taste rather like ginger and are used in Indonesian cooking.

Lesser *galangal (Alpinia officinarum)* is the rhizome of a plant native to China. Its roots have a pepper-ginger flavour and are used in many Indonesian and Malaysian dishes. In Indonesia, it is also known as *laos. Laos* or *galangal* can occasionally be obtained fresh from Asian grocers. Peel and slice it before use. If unavailable, substitute fresh ginger, although the taste is not the same.

GARAM MASALA

A blend of dry-roasted and ground spices well-used in Indian cuisine. The spices used for *garam masala* warm the body (*garam* means warm). Such spices include dried chilies, black pepper, cardamom, coriander, cinnamon, cloves and cumin. Other spices, such as ajowan, mace, nutmeg, fennel, bay leaves, ginger, and white and green pepper, as well as other ingredients such as sesame seeds, coconut and saffron, are also used according to the region, since Indian cooking styles vary immensely according to the geographical location. Generally, garam masala is added towards the end of cooking. Various *garam masalas* can be purchased at Indian grocery stores.

GHEE

The oil produced by clarifying butter over gentle heat until all the moisture is driven off and the milk solids are fully separated from the clear butterfat. The essential difference between ghee and clarified butter, or butter oil, is that in the preparation of ghee, the solids (milk proteins and salts) are allowed to brown before being removed, thus imparting a nutty flavour. Ghee is an excellent choice for sautéeing and frying, and is much favoured in Indian cooking, as well as some French, Saudi Arabian and other Middle Eastern cuisines. Ghee can be purchased at Indian or Middle Eastern grocery stores or some well-stocked supermarkets.

GINGER

The thick white tuberous underground stems or rhizomes of the plant *Zingiber officinale*. Fresh ginger root has a spicy, sweet aroma and a hot, clean taste and is used in many cuisines, especially throughout China, Japan, Thailand and India. The young "green" ginger is especially appreciated for its fibre-free texture and mild flavour. Mature ginger root is more readily available at produce markets, Asian grocery stores and some supermarkets.

Fresh ginger should be peeled before

use. It can be minced, sliced, puréed, shredded or cut into julienne strips and used in vegetable dishes, dals and soups, savouries, fried dishes, chutneys, rices, sweets and drinks.

GLUTINOUS RICE

Also known as sticky rice, glutinous rice can either be white or black, short or long grain. The Chinese and Japanese prefer the short grain variety, while in Thailand, long grain glutinous rice is preferred. White sticky rice is used primarily in sweet dishes throughout Asia, with the exception being the mountain areas of northern Thailand, Cambodia and Laos, where long grain sticky rice is the staple.

HARICOT BEANS

A member of the *Phaseolus vulgaris* species, which includes not only haricot, but kidney beans, great Northern beans and pinto beans. These dried white beans are popular in soups, stews and casseroles. They are well-used in Italian cooking and are known as *fagiolo secco*. They are available at grocery stores and supermarkets.

HING
(See **ASAFETIDA**)

INARI SKIN

Also known as *abura-age-dofu*. Deep-fried tofu slices that are stuffed with flavoured *sushi* rice to prepare the well-known sweet-savoury Japanese finger food *inari-zushi*. Since it is not possible to prepare *abura-age-dofu* at home, you will

need to obtain them from well-stocked Asian grocers, where they come either in shrink-wrapped pouches or in cans.

(TO) INFUSE

To steep, or heat gently to extract flavour.

HORSERADISH ROOT

The root of the hardy perennial plant *Armoracia rusticana*. When scraped or bruised, these stout, white, fleshy, cylindrical roots emit their characteristic highly pungent, penetrating odour, plus volatile oils which cause tears to flow. Horseradish roots are generally peeled and grated and made into sauces to accompany savoury dishes. When choosing horseradish select large roots. The inside core is woody and is not used. Shred or grate the outside of the root, but use straight away and do not cook it, or else the pungent flavour will fade.

Dehydrated powdered horseradish can be used as a substitute, but fresh is better. Fresh horseradish root is sometimes available at quality produce markets and greengrocer shops. The powdered horseradish is available at specialty shops and some supermarkets.

JAGGERY

An unrefined sugar made from the juice crushed out of sugar cane stalks. The juice is boiled down to about a quarter of its original volume into thick brown syrup. As the syrup thickens further and more liquid evaporates, it is scooped out and placed on palm leaves to harden.

MUSTARD SEEDS

Of the many varieties of mustard, three are most prominent. The tiny, round, brownish-black seeds from the plant known as *Brassica nigra,* commonly known as black mustard, the purple-brown seeds of *Brassica juncea,* commonly called brown mustard, and the yellow seeds from *Brassica alba,* known as white or yellow mustard.

Black and brown mustard seeds are often confused with one another. Brown mustard seeds, *Brassica juncea,* are commonly used as a spice seed in Indian cuisine where they are known as *rai.* In South Indian cuisine they are fried in hot oil or ghee to extract their nutty, pungent flavour before being added to soups, chutneys or vegetables dishes. In Bengali cuisine, mustard seeds are one of the five ingredients in the whole spice blend known as panch puran. Yellow mustard seeds (Brassica alba), are less pungent than the darker varieties and are commonly used in European cuisine as a pickling spice. They are strongly preservative, discouraging moulds and bacteria, hence their inclusion in pickles.

When mustard seeds are pounded, they form the basis of immense varieties of commercial brands of the condiment known as mustard. Different varieties of mustard are made from different combinations of hulled and unhulled yellow or brown seeds. It is interesting to note that the pungency of mustard is due to an essential oil which is not present in the seed or the powder, but which forms when the crushed seed is mixed with water. An enzyme then causes a bitter substance in the seed to react with the water, and the hot taste of the mustard emerges. Yellow mustard seeds are available from supermarkets and grocers, and brown or black mustard seeds are available at Indian grocery stores.

NIGELLA SEEDS
(See KALONJI)

NUTMEG

The fragrant nut found in the centre of the fruit of the densely foliated evergreen tree Myristica fragrans. The fleshy fruit of the nutmeg tree resembles an apricot. When it is ripe, it splits in half, revealing the beautiful, brilliant scarlet, net-like membrane, or avil, known as mace. It closely enwraps a brittle shell containing the glossy-brown oily nutmeg. Nutmeg is egg-shaped, and is about 2.5 cm (1 inch) in diameter, with a sweet, warm, and highly spicy flavour.

Nutmeg is used in many cuisines of the world. It is often an ingredient in the North Indian spice blend known as *garam masala,* and is used in cakes and sweet dishes. It is wonderful with pumpkin, squash and sweet potato. In Italian cuisine, it is very popular in spinach dishes and combines well with cheese. Nutmeg is also a common flavouring in the Levant and in various spicy dishes of South East Asia.

Whole nutmegs are best ground straight into the dish in which they are being used, as once grated nutmeg quickly loses its flavour. Whole nutmegs are available at specialty stores and well-stocked supermarkets and grocery stores.

OAT BRAN

The fibre-rich, coarse layer removed from under the outer husk of oats, during the early stages of milling. Oat bran is a good source of iron, thiamine and niacin.

OATMEAL

The hulled oat grain that has been rolled or cut into flakes. There are three basic types: quick-cook or rolled oats, which generally has small flakes, hulled or gritted oatmeal, and steel-cut oatmeal. Oatmeal is among the most nutritious of all the grains. It is 16.7 per cent protein, and is rich in inositol (one of the B-complex vitamins), iron, phosphorus and thiamine. Oatmeal is generally used as porridge or muesli, but is also baked in breads and savoury dishes. It is available at any grocery store.

OLIVE OIL

The oil extracted from the fruits of the Mediterranean tree, *Olea europaea.* The finest olive oil is cold-pressed from fresh, ripe olives and has a pale-yellow or greenish colour and a very delicate flavour. Cruder versions of olive oil are second pressings made under heat. I prefer to have at least two grades of olive oil in the kitchen; mild, cold-pressed, extra-virgin olive oil for salads and uncooked dishes, and a pure, lighter grade olive oil with a high smoking-point for cooking.

Choosing olive oil is much a matter of personal taste and preference. Olive oil is used in many cuisines of the world, not only in Mediterranean cooking. Good quality olive oil is available at specialty and continental grocers and well-stocked supermarkets.

OREGANO

A piquant herb famous in Greek and Italian cuisine. Oregano is botanically confused with marjoram. In fact, for many years both marjoram and oregano were known as *Marjorana hortensis*. There is still confusion today — oregano is still sometimes known as "wild marjoram".

Generally, what is purchased as oregano today is most probably *Oreganum vulgare,* with a strong, piquant, sweet flavour and a pleasantly bitter, aromatic undertone.

Oregano is excellent with any tomato dish, especially pizza and varieties of tomato dishes that include pasta sauces. Its flavour marries well with basil. Oregano is available at any Continental grocer, supermarket or specialty shop.

PALM SUGAR

A dark brown sugar produced by boiling down the sap of various palm trees. Palm sugar has a rich, sweet taste and is an appropriate sweetener in various South East Asian and Indonesian dishes. It is sold in thick, tubular sections or round lumps and is available from Asian grocers.

(TO) PAN-FRY

The technique of frying any ingredient in a small amount of oil.

PANIR

(See **CURD CHEESE**)

PAPRIKA

The bright red powder made from the dried, sweet chili-pepper pods of the many varieties of *Capsicum annuum*. Good paprika has a brilliant red colour and because it is not hot, it can be used in generous quantities, giving dishes a rich, red hue. It is also very nutritious, having a high vitamin C content.

Paprika is the national spice of Hungary, and is featured in Hungarian and Spanish, as well as North Indian cuisines, where it is used in dals and sauces. It is available at grocery stores.

PARMESAN

The most famous of all the grana or matured hard cheeses of Italy. Parmesan or *parmigiano,* takes at least two years to come to maturity, resulting in its traditional sharp flavour. Parmesan cheese should be bought in pieces, to be freshly grated over sauces, pasta or rice or added to cooked dishes.

PARSLEY

One of the best known and most extensively used culinary herbs in Western cuisine. There are numerous cultivated varieties of parsley, but the ornamental curled variety is most popular as a garnish, and the flat-leaved parsley is most favoured in Italian and other Mediterranean cuisines. Both are varieties of *Petroselinum crispum*. Healthful parsley leaves, with their familiar, mild, agreeable flavour, are an excellent source of vitamin C, iron, iodine and other minerals. Parsley is appealing to the eye, nose, and taste, will sweeten the breath, and is a natural herbal deodoriser. It is a pleasant addition to an enormous variety of savoury dishes. It is available at produce markets, green grocers and supermarkets.

PEPPER

The small round berries of the woody, perennial, evergreen vine, *Piper nigrum*. Black pepper, white pepper and green pepper are also obtained from these same berries at different stages of maturity. For black pepper, the berries are picked while green, left in heaps to ferment, sundried and allowed to shrivel and turn dark brown or black. Thus the whole berry, including the dark outer hull, forms what we know as black pepper.

White pepper is produced from fully ripened berries, which are greenish-yellow when picked and at the point of turning red. Then they are soaked in water, the outer hull is rubbed off, and the grey inner berries are sun dried until they turn creamy white, to become what is known as white pepper.

Green peppercorns are soft, immature berries that have been picked and preserved in brine or freeze-dried. Black pepper is characterised by a penetrating odour and a hot, biting, and extremely pungent flavour; milder flavoured white pepper is generally appreciated in European cuisine. Either way, black and white pepper are used in practically every cuisine in the world. Although available pre-ground, discerning cooks prefer the superior flavour of freshly ground peppercorns, for which a pepper mill is an essential acquisition.

PESTO

Referred to as *pistou* in France, the famous pungent sauce made primarily of fresh basil leaves, parmesan cheese and toasted pine nuts.

primarily of fresh basil leaves, parmesan cheese and toasted pine nuts.

PINE NUTS

Also known as pine kernels, *pignolia* or *pinoli*. Pine nuts come from the Stone Pine, *Pineus pinea,* a beautiful Mediterranean pine tree. The pine cones are gathered, the seeds shaken out and cracked, and the small white or cream-coloured kernels are extracted. Their delicious, delicate nutty taste has made them a very popular ingredient in Italian, Spanish and Middle Eastern cuisine. They are available at specialty, Continental or Middle Eastern groceries.

POLENTA

A yellow maize, or cornmeal grown in Northern Italy, where it is regarded as a staple food. Polenta is graded according to its texture and is available fine, medium or coarse-ground. It is available at most supermarkets and health food stores.

POMEGRANATE MOLASSES

A thick, dark and sour syrup produced from boiling down pomegranate juice. Used for flavouring various Middle Eastern dishes. Available at Middle Eastern grocers, it is not to be confused with pomegranate syrup (grenadine) which is sweet.

POPPY SEEDS

Two varieties of poppy seed are referred to here: black and white. Both are seeds of the poppy plant *Papaver somniferum.* The minute, kidney-shaped, bluish-black seeds have a pleasant nutty taste and crunchy texture. They are well-known in Middle Eastern and

European cuisine as a topping for breads and cakes or ground up and sweetened as a pastry filling. White poppy seeds are much used in Indian cuisines. They are even smaller than black poppy seeds, have a similar flavour and are creamy-white. When ground, they add special flavours to Bengali dishes. They are especially used as a thickener for sauces or gravies. (Flours are generally not used in Indian cuisine for this purpose.) Obtain black poppy seeds from any grocer or supermarket. White poppy seeds can be purchased at Indian grocers.

PRASADAM

Food that has been offered to God before being eaten. *Prasadam* means "God's mercy".

PULAO

The terms *pulao, pilau* and *pilaf* refer to classical rice dishes where dry rice is fried in oil or butter until it becomes translucent before liquid is added. The oil impregnates the outer layers of the grains and helps keep them separate while cooking.

RADICCHIO

A crunchy-textured salad green with a refreshingly bitter flavour. The most common variety has a spherical head and reddish-purple leaves with creamy-white ribs. When selecting radicchio, look for a compact head with fresh leaves without brown spots. Store in an upright container in the crisper section of the refrigerator.

RAU RAM
(See **VIETNAMESE MINT**)

RENNET

Rennet is an enzyme used in cheese making which coagulates milk proteins, thus setting the curd. The first step in cheese making is the addition of a starter culture of *Streptococci* and *Lactobacilli.* These bacteria ferment the lactose to lactic acid and reduce the milk's pH to the proper range for the rennet to coagulate the proteins. The rennet is added at this stage. The active enzyme in rennet, called rennin, is remarkably efficient. In pure form, one part will coagulate 5 million parts of milk.

The problem for strict vegetarians is that most cheese manufacturers use a rennet derived from the fourth, or true stomach of a milk-fed calf. The good news is that although calves' stomachs are the classic source of rennet, there are alternatives. Many cheeses produced in Australia now come with "non-animal rennet" listed with the ingredients. That means the manufacturers have used herbal, microbial or synthetic rennet to make their cheese.

RICOTTA CHEESE

Crumbly, soft, white cheese made from the whey of cow's milk and popular in Italian cuisine. It is frequently used in cooking both sweet and savoury dishes in Italy, for like curd cheese or cottage cheese its mild, somewhat bland flavour combines well with other ingredients. It is available at selected supermarkets or grocers.

RIGANI

Greek or wild oregano is a stronger, sharper version of the familiar Italian herb. *Rigani* is sold dried in large bunches in Greek stores. It is worth seeking out to give an authentic flavour to Greek recipes. Italian oregano can be substituted, but the flavour will not be as authentic.

RISOTTO

The rice eaten throughout Northern Italy. Authentic risotto should be prepared only with an Italian superfino rice, such as arborio rice. In risotto cooking, the rice is first coated in butter, then cooked slowly with the gradual addition of stock, and stirred continuously until the stock is absorbed and the rice is soft, with a gentle coating of sauce.

ROCKET
(See **ARUGULA**)

ROSEMARY

The small, narrow, aromatic leaves of the evergreen shrub, *Rosmarinus officinalis*. This fragrant seasoning herb with its clean, woody odour reminiscent of pine, is popular in some European cuisines. Its strong, camphor-like taste is not always appreciated, however, and it is easily overused. Because whole leaves of dried rosemary are not pleasant to find in a dish, I find it useful to grind them to a powder before using. If fresh rosemary is available, whole sprigs can be added to a dish and removed at the completion of the cooking.

ROSE WATER

The diluted essence of rose petals, particularly from the highly scented species *Rosa damascena* and *Rosa centifolia*. It is widely used throughout the Middle East and India as a flavouring agent. It is available at Middle Eastern and Indian grocers.

RYE FLOUR

A flour made from milled rye, popular for bread making.

SAFFRON

The slender dried stigmas of the flowers of *Crocus sativus,* grown commercially in Spain, Kashmir and China. When the plants bloom, the brilliant stigmas, the flower parts that collect pollen, are hand-picked daily, just as the plants open in the early morning. About 210,000 dried stigmas, picked from about 70,000 flowers, yield half a kilo of saffron. Understandably, the cost of saffron production is very high, and saffron is the worldís most expensive spice. Prices range from $3,000 to $5,000 per kilo.

After picking, the saffron is dried in sieves over low heat, then stored immediately. The final product is a compressed, highly aromatic, matted mass of narrow, thread-like, dark-orange to reddish-brown strands, about 2.5 cm (1-inch) long.

Saffron has a pleasantly spicy, pungent, slightly bitter, honey-like taste, with such a potent colouring power that one part of its colouring component, known as crocin, is capable of colouring up to 150,000 parts of water unmistakably yellow.

Saffron has enjoyed immense popularity throughout the world for centuries. By the sixteenth century, for instance, saffron was being extensively cultivated in England as a culinary spice. Its popularity today is limited to mainly Indian, French, Middle Eastern and Spanish cuisines. Saffron strands should be soaked and ground or slightly dry-

roasted and powdered before using. A big pinch of saffron is sufficient to colour a whole dish, but be sure to purchase the real thing ó saffron is often adulterated. And remember, there is no such thing as cheap saffron! Saffron is available at Indian grocers, gourmet stores and large Chinese medical centres where it is known as hoong fa (ask for the more expensive variety).

SAHLEP

A powder derived from the *Sahlep* orchid, *Orchis mascula*. It makes a delicious hot drink when added to milk. Sahlep powder is available from Turkish or Middle Eastern grocery stores.

SALSA

The word salsa literally means "sauce" in Spanish. Outside of Spanish-speaking countries, it usually refers to a sauce or relish made with freshly chopped, uncooked ingredients, usually tomatoes, a herb, fresh chilies and sometimes a little lime or lemon juice.

SAMBAL OELEK

A hot condiment made from ground, fresh, hot red chilies, popular in Malay and Indonesian cuisine. It is often added to a dish for an extra hot chili dimension or served as an accompaniment. Available at Asian grocery stores.

To make 2 teaspoons of your own sambal oelek, pound together two hot red chilies and ½ teaspoon salt.

SAMBAR MASALA

A zesty South Indian spice combination always added to the famous hot- and-sour dal dish called *sambar.*

SEMOLINA

The cream-coloured cereal obtained from hard durum wheat grains in the middle stages of flour milling, when the wheat germ, bran and endosperm are separated. The first millings of the endosperm are known as semolina. Semolina is ground fine, medium and coarse. Besides being used for making pasta in Italy, where semolina enjoys great popularity, it is also used in Indian cuisine, where it is known as sooji. It is simmered for fluffy, sweet halava puddings or savoury vegetable dishes called upma. I find that medium or coarse-ground semolina yields the best semolina halava. Semolina is available at Indian, Italian or specialty grocers and supermarkets.

SESAME SEEDS

The seeds of the cultivated annual plant, Sesamum indicum, grown predominantly in India and China. These flat, pear-shaped seeds are generally lightly roasted to bring out their nutty flavour and are popular in many cuisines of the world. In Western cuisine, they are scattered on breads and cakes before baking. They are ground into a delicious Middle Eastern confection called halva and a semi-liquid paste called tahini. In Japanese cuisine they are roasted with sea salt and ground to a fine powder called gomashio, a versatile condiment; and they are popular in many regional Indian cuisines.

STAR ANISE

The dried, hard, brown and star-shaped fruit of the small evergreen tree, Illicium verum. Star anise has a delicate, dry, spicy, woody, anise-like flavour and odour, and is an ingredient in the Chinese five-spice powder. It is delicious in chutneys, savoury dishes and in poached fruits. It is available at well-stocked gourmet or Indian grocers.

SNAKE BEANS

Known by various names, including asparagus bean, Chinese long bean and yard bean. These narrow, round-bodied beans are dark green, stringless and approximately 30 – 40 centimetres (12 – 16 inches) in length. They taste similar to green beans, but have a denser texture. Choose slender, crisp, bright-green beans, with no blemishes or signs of yellowing. They are best stored wrapped in plastic in the refrigerator. Available at Indian and Asian vegetable markets and well-stocked supermarkets.

SORREL

The word sorrel is derived from the old teutonic word for sour. Sorrel, which shares the same family as rhubarb, has a refreshing, somewhat bitter, sour, spinach-like flavour. It should always be cooked for a minimum time to preserve its fresh flavour. If used raw in salads, select only young, tender leaves.

MUNG BEAN SPROUTS

Sprouted, whole green mung beans. In Chinese cooking, the mung beans are allowed to sprout until quite long. However, from a nutritional point of view, mung beans are best used when the beans have just sprouted and the shoot is less than 1 cm long. Sprouted mung beans are crisp in texture and bursting with nutrition. In Indian cuisine, these barely-sprouted beans are favoured. Theyíre rich in vitamins B, C and E.

Sprouted mung beans are 37 per cent protein (their protein content is highly digestible). They are pleasantly sweet, low in calories and inexpensive.

SRILA PRABHUPADA

The Founder-Acarya (spiritual master) of the International Society for Krishna Consciousness (ISKCON). His Divine Grace A.C. Bhaktivedanta Swami Prabhupada was the author of many spiritual texts and the world's most distinguished teacher of Vedic religion and thought. He guided his Society and saw it grow to a worldwide confederation of hundreds of asramas, schools, temples, institutes and farm communities.

SUMAC

An important souring agent in Arab cuisine. The seeds of Rhus corioria are ground to a purple-red powder and used to add a sour, pleasantly astringent taste to recipes as a preferred substitute for lemon. Sumac's pleasant, rounded, fruity sourness whish is well worth experimenting with.

SUNFLOWER SEEDS

The tightly packed core of sunflowers yields small oval-shaped off-white to grey-coloured kernels. They are firm in texture with a nutty crunch and are rich in protein (23 per cent). They are also a good source of zinc, iron, potassium and magnesium. Sunflower seeds are a versatile kitchen ingredient and are equally great in salads, pasta dishes, cereals and breads. Available at most supermarkets or health food stores.

SUSHI VINEGAR
A mild tasting vinegar made from rice that is specifically made for sushi. Other vinegars cannot be substituted, as they are too strong.

TAHINI
A semi-liquid sesame butter used in Middle Eastern cuisine. This cream-grey paste has the consistency of runny peanut butter and is the basis of various salad dressings and *mezze* (entrées) throughout Greece, Cyprus, Lebanon, Jordan and Syria, where it is known as *tahina*.

TAMARIND
The pulp extracted from the brown pods of the tamarind tree, *Tamarindus indica*. The fresh pulp has a sour, fruity taste and is popular in Indian and Indonesian cooking. Tamarind is available in different forms commercially. The crudest consists of blocks of partly dried, unpitted, broken, sticky fibrous pods. They should be macerated in water to extract the sour, brown tamarind juice, as should blocks of seedless tamarind. The most convenient is tamarind concentrate, which can be used straight from the jar. Tamarind makes excellent sweet and sour chutneys or sauces and can be used in vegetable dishes and curries. Tamarind in its various forms is available at Indian and South-East Asian grocery stores.

TEMPE
Yellow-brown cakes of compressed, culture-inoculated fermented whole soya beans. A white soft coating, similar to that which covers cheese like brie or camambert, forms over the cakes, holding the grains together. The texture of tempe is soft-crunchy, and nutritionally, tempe is high in easily assimilated proteins and low in cholesterol. Tempe is particularly popular in Indonesian cuisine.

THAI BASIL
Also known as *bai horapa*. It is a popular ingredient in Vietnamese, Thai and Chinese cookery. It is easily distinguished from sweet basil by its deep-purple stems and purple-tinged leaves, and has a more pungent, slightly anise flavour. Store it standing upright in a container of water at room temperature. Available at Asian green grocers.

THAI RICE
A long-grained, aromatic white rice from Thailand. Sometimes called jasmine rice, it cooks to large, soft, fluffy grains.

THYME
This attractive herb is grown in Mediterranean regions and Asia Minor. There are more than 100 species of thyme, but common or garden thyme, *Thymus vulgaris,* is frequently used. Others include lemon, mint, orange, golden-lemon, caraway-scented, woolly-stemmed, and the silver thyme. Used fresh or dried, thyme imparts a distinctively warm, pleasant, aromatic flavour and is popular as one of the great European culinary herbs. It is used alongside bay and parsley in bouquet garni, and goes into many soups and vegetable dishes, especially potatoes, zucchini, eggplant and sweet peppers. It is available fresh at selected greengrocers and dried at grocery stores and supermarkets.

TOFU
Soy bean curd or tofu is used in Chinese, Japanese, Korean and Indonesian cooking. This white, almost tasteless and odourless substance is produced from soya beans that have been successively crushed, boiled in water, strained and pressed into a mould. Tofu is low in calories and is cholesterol-free. High in protein, tofu is becoming increasingly popular in Western kitchens. Standard Chinese tofu, which is lightly pressed, is sold fresh in most Chinese grocers. It has the consistency of firm custard. A firmer variety of tofu is also available in Chinese shops and health food stores. This variety is good for slicing, cubing and deep-frying.

TOOR DAL
Also known as *arhar dal, toovar dal* or pigeon peas, these cream-coloured split lentils, which are paler in colour, flatter and larger than yellow split peas, are widely used for cooking in northern and south western India. They have a delightful, slightly sweet flavour and are easy to digest, especially in the famous South Indian soup-like dishes, *rasam* and *sambar. Toor dal* is available at Indian grocers.

TORTILLA
A thin, round flatbread made from white cornmeal, or masa. Tortillas are the national bread of Mexico and are cooked on a griddle. Theyíre eaten fresh and are also the basis of Mexican dishes such as enchiladas and tacos. Wheat tortillas are used in Mexican cuisine as well.

TREACLE
A sugar by-product produced from

TREACLE

A sugar by-product produced from the liquid remaining after the refined sugar has been crystallised. It is a viscous, dark-brown to black syrup. Its colour and unique flavour make it suitable for baking.

TURMERIC

The rhizome, or underground stem of the tropical herb *Curcuma longa*. The short, waxy, orange-yellow rhizomes are boiled, cleaned, sun dried and then ground to a fine, aromatic, yellowish powder that is used as an essential ingredient in Asian and especially Indian cooking. Turmeric adds a brilliant yellow colour to cooked dishes and imparts a slightly bitter, pungent flavour.

Used in vegetable, legume, bean and dal dishes, it introduces colour and warmth to a dish, although overuse produces excessive colour and bitterness. Turmeric powder is available at Indian grocers and specialty stores. Fresh turmeric root is becoming more easily available in Asian stores. The most common is red turmeric *(Zingiber curcuma longa)*. These small roots need to be scraped or carefully peeled to expose the deep burnt-orange flesh. Crushed in a mortar and pestle or grated, they form the basis of curry pastes, especially in Thai cuisine. I have used fresh turmeric root in rice with delicious results, as well as chopped finely in dals and soups. Fresh turmeric is available seasonally from well-stocked Asian grocers.

URAD DAL

The split dried beans from the plant *Phaseolus mungo*. Whole *urad* beans are blackish-grey. Split *urad dal* are cream-white. Their shape resembles their close relative, split mung *dal*. They are used to prepare protein-rich purées and soups in Indian cuisine, and when combined with grains and milk products, their protein value increases. In South Indian cooking, they are fried in ghee or oil for use as a nutty seasoning and soaked and ground into dumplings, pancakes and fried savouries. *Urad dal* is available at Indian grocery stores.

VANILLA

The pod of the climbing tropical orchid, *Vanilla planifolia*. The vanilla flavouring material is obtained from the dried, cured, partially ripe pods. The white crystalline compound called vanillin, present only in the cured black pods, provides the delicately sweet, rich, spicy and persistent aroma which characterises vanilla. Whole vanilla beans are cooked with creams, custards and sauces in French cuisine. The beans can be washed, dried and re-used. Vanilla sugar and pure vanilla essence are substitutes. Vanilla beans are available at specialty grocers.

VIETNAMESE MINT

This pungent flavoured herb is not a true mint, but widely known by this common name. It is also known as Cambodian mint, hot mint, *laksa leaf, daun laksa,* and *daun kesom*. It is easily available from Vietnamese grocers where it is known as *rau ram*. The leaves are narrow and pointed with distinctive dark markings in the centre. In Vietnamese cooking, the herb is not cooked but used in salads or eaten as a fresh accompaniment to the well-known Vietnamese spring rolls.

VINE LEAVES

The leaves of the grape vine *Vitis vinifera*. The most popular use of vine leaves in vegetarian cookery is to stuff them with aromatic rice. The resultant little parcels are enjoyed in Middle Eastern and Mediterranean cuisines as dolma or dolmades. Vine leaves are obtained fresh in countries where grapes grow (leaves from any vine yielding edible grapes are suitable) or purchased preserved in water, salt, and citric acid in jars or plastic pouches from Greek or Middle Eastern grocery stores.

WATER CHESTNUTS

Fresh water chestnuts, with their crunchy, succulent texture and sweet, nutty taste, are a common delicacy in Asian cuisine. They are actually the edible roots of an aquatic plant. The fresh water chestnut has a tight skin, and should be peeled and sliced as required. If unavailable at good Chinese produce markets, tinned Chinese water chestnuts sold at Chinese grocery stores are an acceptable although inferior-tasting substitute.

WHEY

The liquid by-product when milk is curdled in the curd-cheese making process, or from yoghurt when it is allowed to drain in a cheesecloth. It can be used in bread making, in soups or to cook vegetables. Allowed to sour, it can be used as an agent to curdle further batches of milk.

WILD RICE

Not an actual rice, wild rice *(Zizania aquatica)* is actually an aquatic grass. Since it cooks like rice, and is often mixed with real rice, cookbooks customarily include it in their rice recipe pages. Until recently, wild rice was grown mostly in the lakes and marshes of the northern Great Lakes region of the US and Canada. In 1992, wild rice production began in Australia. Wild rice takes longer to cook than regular rice, and when cooked doubles in size, unlike ordinary rice which quadruples in size. Although wild rice can be cooked for longer periods with extra water to form a very soft fluffy porridge of burst grains, it is traditionally cooked just short of bursting and should be fairly chewy.

YAM BEANS

Known also as sweet turnip as well as by its Mexican name, *jicama* (pronounced hee-kama), a tuber native of tropical America as well as South-East Asia. The Asian variety of yam beans are disc-like with light brown skin and strongly marked segments. Their pleasantly crunchy, white flesh is slightly sweet and juicy and can be eaten raw, like a fruit. Cooked as a vegetable in stir-fried dishes, yam beans make a good substitute for bamboo shoots or especially water chestnuts whose texture is similar. When purchasing yam beans, choose tubers of moderate size with smooth, fine skin, indicating that they are young and fresh.

To prepare yam beans, peel away the skin and slice or dice as required. While their flavour is delicate, they take on other flavours cooked with them. Obtain yam beans from Asian grocers or Latin American stores. Note the regional names for easy purchase: China, *saa got*; Indonesia and Malaysia, *bangkwang*; Philippines, *singkamas*; and Vietnam, *cu san*.

YEAST

Yeast is a single-celled fungus and works in bread by feeding upon the sugars in the dough. Later, it feeds on the maltose produced as starch granules are broken down by malt enzymes. As the yeast metabolises the sugars, it produces carbon dioxide and alcohol, a process in bread making referred to as fermentation.

When the bread is placed in the oven to bake, the carbon dioxide expands in the heat and as it does it enlarges all the little air pockets by stretching the gluten.

Two types of yeast are available for baking bread: dry baking yeast, sometimes called dehydrated or dried yeast; and fresh yeast, sometimes called compressed yeast.

Breweri's and nutritional yeast are not suitable for bread making, since neither have any rising properties.

Note that although dry yeast and fresh yeast are interchangeable in a recipe, you will need about twice the volume of fresh yeast as dried yeast. In other words, if a recipe calls for one teaspoon of dried yeast, you will need about two level teaspoons of fresh yeast.

YOGHURT

This indispensable ingredient in the vegetarian kitchen can be easily made at home by adding a small amount of "starter" (which can be either previously prepared homemade yoghurt or commercial plain yoghurt) to warm milk. When incubated in a warm place for at least four hours, the live bacteria in the starter will transform the milk into yoghurt, which can then be refrigerated and used as needed.

ZEST

The thin, coloured skin of an orange or lemon used to give flavour to various dishes. It is very thinly pared without any of the white bitter pith.

Index

About the Author

Kurma Dasa was born in England, moving to Australia with his parents in 1964. He started his cooking career in the Sydney kitchens of the Hare Krishna movement, where he began by cutting vegetables, grinding fresh herbs and spices, and assisting in the preparation of their famous Sunday Feasts.

Since those humble beginnings, Kurma has gone on to teach his special brand of elegant and eclectic gourmet vegetarian cuisine throughout Australia and around the world.

Kurma was head chef at Melbourne's most popular Vegetarian Restaurant, Gopal's for many years, and is the author of *Great Vegetarian Dishes* (which has been reprinted seven times), *Cooking With Kurma,* and *Quick Vegetarian Dishes*. Kurma's books have received wide acclaim for their professional, clearly written and richly illustrated presentation of vegetarian cuisine.

Kurma has hosted three internationally broadcast television cooking series seen in over 46 countries. His third and latest 26-part TV series *More Great Vegetarian Dishes* recently screened throughout Australia on SBS and Foxtel.

Kurma's light-hearted presentation of healthy, delicious, attractive and innovative cuisine continues to shake off the outdated notion that vegetarian food is dull and lack-lustre. Currently, Kurma is presenting gourmet vegetarian cooking master-classes Australia-wide, writing columns for various magazines, and working on more cookbooks. Kurma lives in Perth.

If you wish to correspond with the author, please write to him at:

PO Box 102 Bayswater, Western Australia 6053, Australia, or

email: kurma@com.org